GHOSTS OF
BRISTOL

GHOSTS OF BRISTOL

HAUNTING TALES FROM THE TWIN CITIES

V.N. "BUD" PHILLIPS

Haunted
America

Published by Haunted America
A Division of The History Press
Charleston, SC 29403
www.historypress.net

Cover images: Front cover image courtesy of Robert White. Back cover image
courtesy of Earl Neikirk.

All images courtesy of the author unless otherwise noted.

First published 2010

Manufactured in the United States

ISBN 978.1.60949.082.9

Library of Congress Cataloging-in-Publication Data

Phillips, V. N. (Victor N.)
Ghosts of Bristol : haunting tales from the Twin Cities / V.N. "Bud" Phillips.
p. cm.
ISBN 978-1-60949-082-9
1. Ghosts--Tennessee--Bristol--Anecdotes. 2. Ghosts--Virginia--Bristol--Anecdotes. 3.
Bristol (Tenn.)--History--Anecdotes. 4. Bristol (Va.)--History--Anecdotes. 5. Bristol (Tenn.)-
-Social life and customs--Anecdotes. 6. Bristol (Va.)--Social life and customs--Anecdotes. 7.
Folklore--Tennessee--Bristol. 8. Folklore--Virginia--Bristol. I. Title.
BF1472.U6P47 2010
133.109768'96--dc22
2010029572

Notice: The information in this book is true and complete to the best of our knowledge. It is
offered without guarantee on the part of the author or The History Press. The author and
The History Press disclaim all liability in connection with the use of this book.

CONTENTS

CONTENTS

PREFACE

Why would a pronounced historical purist write ghost tales? More than once I have faced that question. Basically, it is because of public demand. For several years, I have been pressured to write such a book. In my constant quest for historical information, I have heard hundreds of ghost tales. They seem to be a byproduct of historical research.

ACKNOWLEDGEMENTS

Hundreds of folks have contributed to this work. From my earliest days in Bristol, I began to hear stories of strange and unexplained happenings. And this continued on through the years and has greatly increased during the past decade or so. I owe a big debt to those people who told me those stories through the years. They have supplied the material that you will read here. They have, indeed, made possible this book.

Then there is the mechanical need. Publishers now require a work to be computerized, an art that I have not yet learned. Therefore, I must rely on others. Casey Wilson did the early work of this sort for me. She also gave me much encouragement to begin. Then came Bob White, who brought the manuscript to completion with his computer skills. My greatest outlet for historical writings now is a weekly column in the *Bristol Herald Courier*. I write them all by hand. Then Bob does the computer work, and I am everlastingly grateful for his help. It is also a great benefit to those who regularly read my column.

Then there are numerous people who have and continue to encourage me to keep on writing. To them, and to all others who have helped in any way, I here express my sincere and grateful appreciation.

A BRIEF HISTORY OF BRISTOL

B efore beginning my ghost stories, I think it is fitting that a brief history be given of this city in which these strange and mysterious happenings occurred. Bristol is a unique city, about evenly divided between Tennessee and Virginia. There are actually two versions of its history. One, which I call the "traditional version," is filled with heresy and myth, along with major errors. The other is well documented and based on primary (that is "historically acceptable") sources. The sketch that I will present here is based on primary sources. There are instances where it will vary from the traditional version. When such instances occur, historical claims have been proven wrong and can be verified by comparing documented evidence.

Bristol exists because of two railroads establishing surveys and terminal points at a given location. That location was the plantation of Reverend James King (1791–1867). This plantation, though paid for by Colonel James King, was deeded directly to his son, James King Jr. (later known as Reverend James King). No will was involved, as is claimed by the traditional version. Colonel King's will, made in 1825, was very short, having only sixty-nine words, and there was only one heir mentioned, that being his second wife. All of his property that he wished for the children to have had been given to them long before this will was made.

Malinda, a daughter of Reverend King, married Joseph Rhea Anderson, a successful merchant of Blountville, Tennessee. Mr. Anderson realized that two railroads terminating at a given point would be an ideal location for a town. In 1852, Mr. Anderson laid out the original town of Bristol. This included sections in both Tennessee and Virginia, reaching northward to Beaver Creek.

A first cousin of Reverend James King's, Colonel Samuel E. Goodson, owned a tract of land lying north of Beaver Creek. At some point before 1855, Colonel Goodson laid out a town known as Goodsonville. For about four years, this Goodsonville and the original Bristol, Virginia, existed as adjoining but separate towns. Then, in 1856, a committee of local citizens incorporated a composite town made up of both Bristol and Goodsonville, Virginia. This composite town was known as Goodson. Often, the claim is made that Goodson and Goodsonville were one and the same and that the Goodson land reached all the way to the state line. This is easily shown to be an error by the use of primary sources. Development of the three towns was well on the way when the railroads came into service in 1856 and 1858.

In 1890, the Virginia portion of this city was reincorporated as Bristol. However, bear in mind that this was not the founding of a new town. Sometimes the claim is made that there was no Bristol, Virginia, until 1890. Usually, the additional claim is made that Colonel Samuel E. Goodson founded the town. That is when it becomes a bit amusing. Those of us who stick to primary sources know that the colonel had been dead twenty years by that time!

Be all this as it may, we know that we now have Bristol, Virginia/ Tennessee, and even with all of its supposed frightful ghosts, it is still a *very* good place to live.

PART I

FROM THE PAST:
HAUNTS FROM EARLY BRISTOL

BRISTOL'S FIRST KNOWN GHOST

I have many stories of ghosts that were encountered in the Bristol area long before a town developed here. Here is the story of the first known ghost to appear after the new town of Bristol, Virginia/Tennessee, was founded in 1852. This happened in late 1854, and the site is near where Winston's Alley now enters Lee Street.

In 1853, John H. Moore, formerly of Russell County, Virginia, bought a choice lot in Bristol, Virginia, located on the northwest corner of Lee and State Streets. On it he soon erected the second store to operate in Bristol, Virginia, and the third in the entire town. His residence was actually an extension of the store. Near the back of the lot was a small smokehouse.

At first, the Moores' water supply was a cistern located near their back door. But in late 1854, they hired a local "water witch" to locate a promising well site in the home yard. The location was to the left of the little smokehouse. At the dawning of a November morning in 1854, Mrs. Moore took a large butcher knife and started toward the smokehouse, planning to slice off bacon for breakfast. At the back steps, just as she was entering the walk that led to the smokehouse, she froze in her tracks, horrified. She saw a large and very tall Indian warrior standing just to the left of the smokehouse. In one hand he held a tomahawk high and was

This downtown building, erected in 1898, now covers the lot where Bristol's first known ghost appeared.

swinging it as if ready to attack. With the other hand, he was pointing toward the stake that marked the new well site. His head was shaking as if to indicate "No!" and his face was contorted as if in extreme anger. But as the terrified Mrs. Moore stared directly at him for long moments, the Indian just suddenly vanished into thin air. He was never seen again. Everything was back to normal. Even so, Mrs. Moore would not proceed on to the smokehouse. There would be no bacon for breakfast.

Now, to add to the mystery, the large butcher knife that Mrs. Moore had carried outside had disappeared and was never found. I wonder if she threw it at the Indian and it was lost in the grass. Or by some mysterious power did the Indian seize it and take it from this plane? We'll never know. All we know is that they searched but never found that butcher knife.

A few days later, even though Mrs. Moore was protesting that she believed they should not proceed with the digging of the well—thinking that this appearance of the Indian pointing to the spot and shaking his head "No!" in great agitation and anger meant that something was wrong—Mr. Moore would not give in to superstitions and had his men go right ahead and dig the well. When they were some six feet down, they dug into an Indian grave and there found a skeleton of a very tall and large man. Well now, Mr. Moore was immediately convinced and had the spot filled up. Everything became peaceful again. The Moores continued using the cistern for the time they remained in Bristol.

So, folks, that was the first known ghost to appear in Bristol, Virginia/Tennessee.

The Ghost of Doug Thomas

Competition was so keen among early Bristol merchants that most stores were opened by 6:00 a.m. and did not close until at least 8:00 p.m. Colonel J.M. Barker, an early and prominent merchant here, kept such hours in his store. He had a large, three-story building on the Virginia side of Bristol in the 500 block of Main (State) Street. Lighting in all local stores of the period was very dim. Some had oil lamps, while a few still resorted to multiple candles. These were called "candle clusters" by most of the people of that day and time. Colonel Barker had both.

Deep snow lay on the ground on that cold, late afternoon on January 16, 1880. But this did not prevent a man and his wife from trudging from their home a mile or so west of town to Barker's store. The colonel was the only one in the store at that time. He had lost his chief clerk, young Doug Thomas, in a sad tragedy just before Christmas. An angry man by the last name of Rader had murdered poor Thomas and had cut his throat from ear to ear, causing him to bleed to death on the floor of a drugstore next door to Barker's. As this tragic event had happened only weeks before, a sad pall still hung over the town and that store.

Once inside the store, the man went to the men's boot section, while his wife began making a selection in the lady's department. If no lady clerk was available in those days, a woman was usually left alone to make her own selections. It was considered improper for a man to assist ladies in their choice of wearing apparel, so she sat down in a back section of the store to try on a pair of shoes. Suddenly, the woman let out a bloodcurdling scream, jumped up and, with shoes off, ran out the back door into the cold snow and continued to flee westward toward home. Both Colonel Barker and the much-puzzled husband searched the store

Doug Thomas, a handsome and promising young store clerk, was murdered in Barker's Mercantile Company in December 1879. The appearance of his ghost there led to the demolition of the store building.

for the source of her terror, but nothing could be found. Finally, the husband, carrying her abandoned shoes in his hand, hurried home. He found his wife in bed, a quilt covering her head and ears, still quaking in fear. It was far into the night before he got her calmed down enough to tell her frightful story.

Both she and her husband had been well acquainted with young Doug Thomas. As she sat there that evening in Barker's dimly lit store, trying to make a shoe selection, she suddenly saw feet approaching her. Strangely, the feet were not taking steps but rather were gliding along slightly above the floor. Startled, she looked up, and there stood Doug Thomas smiling down at her. His white shirt was soaked red with blood, and more was flowing from his slashed throat. One look was enough, and she forgot that she was barefoot and jumped up and ran out the back door through deep snow to her home.

Soon, others began to see this ghostly figure in Barker's big store. At first, the colonel just scoffed at "such nonsense," as he put it. But he had a change of mind soon after when he came to the store before daylight. Just as he entered the store, one of the hanging oil lamps flared up, giving light to the central part of the store. There on a little footstool stood Doug Thomas, stretched up as if he had just completed his usual morning chore, his shirt soaked in blood. It is understandable that the noted Colonel Barker did not open his store that day. Nor did he open the next morning but rather came with a crew and began moving his stock to another building that he owned farther up the street. The haunted store building was never used again, although during the period that it stood there unused, there were reports of strange lights moving about inside the store, and more than one person claimed to see the bloody Doug Thomas peering out the front windows. Even in daylight, people looked the other way when passing the old abandoned store. A little later, the vacant building was demolished, and a smaller building was erected in its place. It was long told that Colonel Barker had a hard time selling even the bricks that were in that building. Folks feared that the ghost of the murdered Doug Thomas might go with them.

The demolition of that building seemed to have ended the ghostly appearance of the poor murdered store clerk. If a thing can happen, it has happened in Bristol! Here we have a ghost who caused a building to be demolished. I have never known of that happening elsewhere.

REVEREND JAMES KING RIDES AGAIN

In the 1850s, there were many wagons, buggies and carts in the Bristol area. There was only one fine carriage, however. That carriage belonged to Reverend James King. At that time, Reverend King was still serving as pastor of the Paperville Presbyterian Church. On those Sundays when he was due there, he oftentimes went by carriage (usually in summertime)— other times he rode horseback. The carriage was pulled by four fine horses and was driven by a faithful slave named Shadrack Wisdom. The carriage route led through Fairmount Forest, and after passing through that forest it followed what was the old Route 421 up to the Jonesboro Road. A left turn was then made on that road, and after passing over the hill a steady decline resulted, all the way to the old brick church where Reverend King was long the pastor.

Reverend James King pastored the Paperville Presbyterian Church for several years. According to late reports, he still sometimes appears there, riding in his grand carriage.

In the summer of 2005, a friend of mine was driving out in that direction. He took the road to the left toward Paperville. As he topped the hill, he saw before him a fine carriage moving rather slowly down the hill toward the church. A black man was seated up front driving the four horses attached to the carriage. Cars were coming in the opposite direction, but people in them did not seem to be aware of the mysterious carriage that was slowly moving before him. When the churchyard was reached, the carriage turned into the parking area. It was then that things really got strange. It appeared that the driver was oblivious to the cars parked there but rather seemed to pass right through them. Then, as my friend watched, those horses, carriage and driver just melted into the church wall and totally disappeared. He didn't know what to make of it. I told him that he seemed to be describing the arrival of Reverend James King at his church long ago. Some local psychic told him that it was a "slip back" in time.

About a year later, a man who attends that church was standing outside waiting on a friend to arrive. He told me that suddenly a strange feeling of coldness ran all over him. Instantly, a fine carriage appeared out in the road and then turned into the parking area. A black man was driving the four horses, and an old gray-haired man was looking out the side window. Evidently, Reverend James King was riding again. Then, just as suddenly as this image appeared, all just disappeared.

I have heard no more of this apparent "slip back" in time, but am truly sorry that I missed it.

PART II

GHOSTS OF THE CIVIL WAR

THE SAD SOLDIER AT CEDAR HILL

Old Cedar Hill Plantation, now commonly known as Painter Place, occupies a particularly beautiful area in the Holston Valley near Bristol, Tennessee. It was originally the home of David King Sr., a pioneer settler from Pennsylvania, who married Elizabeth Sharp, daughter of John Sharp, the pioneer settler of the area. By Civil War times, it had become the property of his son, David O. King II, and his wife, Mariamna McChesney King. The couple's only son, David King III, was a promising young man of unusual intelligence and with a wisdom rarely found in one of his age. When the dreadful Civil War began, he was a student at Tusculum College near Greeneville, Tennessee. Letters to his father at the time show that he felt that it his duty to defend his native South. With this his father fully concurred.

On a sunny, late spring morning in 1861, this father accompanied his son to Bristol, where the latter enrolled as a soldier in the Confederate army. A little later, the father bade his only son goodbye at the Bristol Depot, never to see him again. By June 1862, David King III was in northern Mississippi. Later that month, he was in a forced march through the steamy heat of the central part of that deep Southern state. Somewhere along the line, he became ill and had to spend two or three days in an army hospital. Being very desirous to serve at whatever mission was at hand, he left that hospital before he was really well and continued the march southward. When his company arrived in Canton, Madison County, Mississippi, his condition greatly worsened. He lingered a few days but there died on July 12, 1862. He is buried in the Confederate section of the Old Town Cemetery at Canton, Mississippi (I have twice visited the site).

In some way, word reached Cedar Hill that David O. King's only son was very ill. King immediately started to Mississippi but had some difficulty in reaching the area where his son was being cared for. When he finally arrived in Canton, his son had been dead for over two weeks. It was said that his death was caused by brain fever. It was generally believed that this condition could be brought on by bright sunlight. As a child, I recall being cautioned about going out in the bright sunlight without a hat. Meanwhile, back at Cedar Hill in Sullivan County, Tennessee, the anxious mother awaited news of her husband and son. Weeks passed, and no word was heard from either.

Cedar Hill/Painter Place as it appeared when photographed in the late nineteenth century by Phillip Painter, photographer and descendant. *Collection of Bob White.*

On July 12, 1862, a gentle rain of several hours' duration had fallen on the old Cedar Hill plantation. By twilight, the rain had ceased, and wisps of fog were gently rising here and there on the ridges behind the house and over the dense woodland on the corner of the main field. After supper was finished, Mrs. King left the kitchen cleanup to her daughter Caroline and went to the front porch, where she sat long in an old rocking chair looking out over the home fields, deeply feeling the anxiety that only a soldier's mother could know. Her earnest prayers were going upward for the recovery and future safety of her only son.

As late twilight was becoming dusk, Mrs. King was startled to see a dark figure emerge from the woods at the back corner of the big field and walk slowly toward the house. Looking intently, it appeared that the walk of that person was familiar—and more so as it came closer and closer to the house. It was not until the dark figure reached the home gate that she realized it was her soldier-son, David King III. As she jumped up with shock and joy, her mind tried to comprehend the situation. It couldn't be him, but it was, standing there straight and in full uniform—it was truly him! Had he suddenly recovered and made the long journey home? Was the report of his sickness a mistake? Was her mind playing tricks on her? There he stood, looking over the home gate, still as a statue and looking oh so sad—she would always remember that. She had started to run toward him when he waved to her and then just sunk slowly down into the ground. Speechless, she staggered back to the porch and sank down in her chair. Shocked and saddened to the core, she long sat motionless. She knew what it meant. As dusk turned into a pall of darkness slowly settling over the Cedar Hill Plantation, a dark foreboding set over her troubled mind. She knew what had happened. David was dead. His spirit had come to her, wafted over the more than seven hundred miles between her and Canton, Mississippi. He had come to say goodbye, and she would never see him again. As she would soon learn, her David had died that very day.

For the next several days, she grieved for the loss of her son, as much as if word had already been received telling of his death. Certainly, it was no surprise to her when the long-expected letter arrived from her husband confirming what she had already known. Excerpts from that letter are given here:

Dear wife, I write to you with a sorrowful heart. Our dear, our only son, is dead. He was well treated and decently buried. A lady took him in her carriage every day that he could ride. He was able to walk just four days before he died. He left many messages of love to his mother and to his sisters. I went to his grave and marked the place. Thus, our dream of love is over. We have no son to soothe our age and perpetuate our name. We have a son who has died for his country, whose fame and whose memory is dear to us. He died a victim of duty. He left Enterprise Mississippi before he was well. So anxious was he to do his duty. The march from Tupelo to Alberry killed him. The weather was so hot and he had just got out of the hospital. He was attacked by a fever of the brain and congestive chills and died by degrees, not seeming to suffer much.

A few days after the grieving father returned home, the deceased son appeared to him. It was very late on a summer evening. David O. King had finally taken the old family Bible, retired to the side porch, sat in a crude chair and did what he had so long dreaded to do. Long he had hoped to record in that Bible the marriage of his much-loved son and then one day record his children. Instead, he recorded his untimely death. This he slowly did and then took a sheet of paper and began to write a poem (he was a prolific composer of poems) concerning the death of this only son. The poem he wrote that day long remained between the pages of that Bible:

In the land where the fig and the myrtle appear,
Far from his home, for his Country he died
No father, no mother, no sister was near
No friend, no companion to watch by his side.
On that gloomy night when he struggled alone,
But with none but his Maker to witness his pain
'Ere the morn had arisen his spirit had flown
to the land where peace shall eternally reign.
His likeness is all that I have left to me now.
I can gaze on those features that once were so dear
The intelligent face and that noble brow
I almost imagine that David is here.

But oh, vain delusion, in vain do I seek,
To recall the expression of him I adore.
No breathing is heard. Those lips cannot speak.
Those eyes, so expressive once, sparkle no more.

I will add that the picture he was looking at and referred to so long ago is now in my possession and is kept here at old Pleasant Hill.

The father finished the last line of that poem, and then, mind filled with deep melancholy, he looked long out over the home fields. But then his attention was drawn to the old apple tree in the corner of the backyard. Someone was standing under it. Who could it be? No one had been there just a moment before. Looking closely, he saw that it was David, in full uniform and looking so intently toward the house and so sad. Then he just slowly faded away. David King did not tell his family of this paranormal experience until he was on his deathbed some nineteen years later. Even on that deathbed, there were two or three times when he said that he saw David standing in the room by his bed.

A year after David's death, his sister Caroline (who later married John F. Painter) made an early morning trip to the spring that flowed at a little knoll southwest of the house. (This spring is still flowing and is the head source of what we know as Painter Creek.) The weather was intensely hot, and there had been little cooling during the night, so Caroline wanted to bring in a bucket of fresh drinking water before the sun rose. Daylight was just breaking over the high mountains in the south. About halfway down the path, she met her deceased brother, walking slowly up from the spring. He stopped and she froze in her tracks. He sadly looked intently at her and then rose from the ground a bit and suddenly "faded out," as she would tell so many times in the years after that incident. After her story was told, the father noted that it was one year before, at that very hour, that David had died at Canton, Mississippi.

By seventy years later, the last descendants of the King family to live at Cedar Hill had died or moved away. For a short time, the house stood vacant. Then, in late winter that year, a family of tenant farmers moved in. On a cold, snowy Sunday morning a short time after the family was settled, the husband arose just at daybreak to kindle the fire in the east bedroom in which he and his wife slept. He went back to bed to wait for the room to warm up. He dozed off but within minutes was jerked awake by the screams of his wife. She had awakened and sat up in bed to see just how the fire was doing but saw far more than a roaring fire. A young man in a Civil War uniform was sitting next to the fireplace and was looking intently at her, looking oh so sad. When the husband regained his senses and looked, no one was there. This woman left there that very morning and never returned. They found another house in which to live.

Twenty-two years later (in 1962), the family then living at Cedar Hill (by then long called Painter Place) had relatives in for a few days visit. While there, a number of pictures were made, including several group shots of the resident family and their guests. The film was taken by the visitors to be developed in their hometown. Finally, copies were sent to the relatives at Painter Place, along with the comment that they had completely forgotten that a uniformed soldier had been there that day and was pictured with the group. Sure enough, a soldier was in the picture dressed in a Confederate uniform. The photo was dated July 12, one hundred years to the day since David King III had died in Canton, Madison County, Mississippi.

In the early 1990s, Miss Carrie Painter, then the sole owner of old Cedar Hill Plantation, gave the house and a large lot around it to King College, Bristol, Tennessee. Over the years, it has been rented to several persons and families. One of the renters moved in on July 12. That night, there were strange noises in the south upstairs bedroom. It sounded as if furniture was being moved about with heavy footsteps, which seemed to pace back and forth across the room. Finally, the father of this family steeled his nerves and, with gun in hand, ascended the narrow stairway that leads up from the kitchen. When he reached the hall between the two upstairs bedrooms, the sound suddenly ceased. But then came the sounds of moans and groans, as of someone suffering and dying. He did not long tarry but rather came down the stairs in a hasty manner. Just as he got back to the living room, sounds of someone running down the stairs were clearly heard. The fast-moving steps crossed the kitchen, and as the kitchen door was reached, there appeared in that door a soldier dressed in a uniform that the man of the house did not recognize. Upon describing it to friends, it was Confederate. The bedroom in which the strange sounds were heard was the room occupied by David King as a boy. Strange sounds continued to be heard there by the family, who did not stay very long.

As far as can be determined, there have been no strange happenings at Painter Place in at least ten years. But watch out when July 12 comes again!

Note: For a long time, I hesitated publishing or telling this story for fear that it might create a state of anxiety for those who might occupy the house. Some time ago, I learned that the present occupants of the house are not very much afraid of strange occurrences, and I think they can endure whatever may occur. Having felt the compulsion to tell this for several years, I will tell it by publishing it in this book. Long as it is, it all needed to be told to give it the effect I desired.

THE GEORGIA DRUMMER BOY IN EAST HILL CEMETERY

One hundred or more soldiers are buried in the Confederate section of Bristol's historic East Hill Cemetery. Among them, we know not where, rests the Georgia drummer boy. He joined the service for his beloved Southland when very young. When his true age was discovered, his company was already hundreds of miles from his native Lownds County, Georgia home. Therefore, he was allowed to stay—but not as a regular soldier. He became the drummer boy and, more or less, the favorite of his soldier companions. In time, he became an expert drummer. He was described by old Bristolians as being rather mature for his age (about fifteen), having black hair and piercing black eyes. It was further said that he was one of those rare persons who displayed a perpetual smile.

After traveling with his company for several months, he became ill with some type of fever and was brought to the Confederate hospital in Bristol, Tennessee (this hospital was housed in a former hotel that stood at the southeast corner of what is now State Street and Martin Luther King Boulevard). For a few days, it seemed that he was recovering, but then he became desperately ill. Across the street west of the hospital lived Joseph R. Anderson and family. Aunt Lin, the wife and mother, well known for her innate kindness, learned of the young lad's severe illness and immediately went over to see him (she often went over to visit the sick). In his fevered delirium, the drummer boy mistook her for his own mother and begged her to take him home. Aunt Lin could not refuse such a pathetic plea. She consulted with the superintendent of the

Sometimes faintly, sometimes very loud, the steady beat of the drum can still be heard in East Hill Cemetery coming from a short distance south of the marker pictured here.

hospital and was given permission to move him into her own home. Help was not available, so Aunt Lin carried one end of the stretcher and the superintendent carried the other as the very sick boy was taken across the street. There she had a bed placed in the dining room, where she lovingly gave him care as if she were his own mother. He apparently never knew the difference.

Aunt Lin's mother, Macajah Watkins King, lived two blocks down Main Street. As old and feeble as she was, she often walked to her daughter's home. On her first visit after the sick drummer boy was moved there, she carried a bouquet of pink roses with her. The delirious boy saw them and thought they had been gathered and brought by his own grandmother. Even the color matched the roses grown on his grandmother's rosebush far off in Georgia. It was his last delight on earth. Before night, he lapsed into a deep coma and died shortly before midnight. Late the following afternoon, he was buried among his fallen comrades on the western slope of what is now East Hill Cemetery. Aunt Lin bought a nice casket for him. Her father, the aging Reverend James King, conducted a beautiful funeral service at the graveside (at that time, most of the soldiers were being buried hastily in shallow graves without the benefit of caskets or funeral services). The roses brought by Mrs. Mourning Macajah Watkins King the day before were lovingly placed on his grave.

Gideon Burkhart, Bristol's first lawyer, attended the funeral. He then went on to Paperville to see relatives there. He visited longer than he planned, so it was well past dark when he began his journey home. As he neared the new town cemetery, he was startled to hear the distinct sound of a drumbeat coming from the section where the Confederate soldiers were buried. Now, most Bristolians of the time would have arrived quicker at home than they planned if they had heard such commotion, but not Gideon. He was a very brave man, and there was not a superstitious bone in him. He had long been the type to investigate any strange thing rather than to flee from it. He reined in his horse, dismounted and walked right into the darkened cemetery. As he approached the Confederate section, the drumbeat grew louder and seemed to be coming from the area of the newly made grave of the Georgia drummer boy. In moments, the ground began to tremble and the beat became deafening. It was then that the brave lawyer decided that he would no longer tarry. After he told the story and admitted to leaving the cemetery, someone asked him if he ran. In his own droll way, he replied that he did not run but might have attained a pretty good trot before he reached his horse. He told that he continued to hear the drumbeat all the way to the railroad crossing. Strangely, others who lived nearby did not hear it.

From time to time over the years, others told of hearing the mysterious drumbeat in the soldier's section of the cemetery. One notable incident was still remembered by a few older local residents when I arrived here in 1953. About 1905, the annual memorial service was being held in the cemetery. Part of that service was always dedicated to memorializing the fallen soldiers. Major Henry C. Wood was the speaker for that part of the program that day. He well knew the story of the drummer boy and was including him in his lavish praise for the faithful fallen comrades. In the midst of the Major's speech, the faint sound of a drumbeat was heard, first seemingly far off but then coming closer. Many in the crowd left the scene rather hastily, but several, including Major Wood and other Confederate veterans, simply stood in awe. They knew that they were hearing a sound from Civil War days repeated after the passage of nearly forty years. They considered this to be almost a spiritual occurrence. The drumbeat finally faded out, and this ended the memorial service that year. Those who had remained just walked silently away.

Two or three times during the years that have passed since I've been here, I have had reports of a mysterious drumbeat being heard in this old cemetery. No one knows when it may happen again.

THE GHOST THAT WASN'T

The following story was told to me by Ol' Dad Thomas. He was six years old and present when the event occurred. He said that it was the clearest memory he had of the Civil War period. What he didn't remember, his mother had told him, making it possible for him to give a very detailed account of this event long ago.

An old pre–Civil War house stood on Washington Street until perhaps twenty years ago. I was very familiar with it and visited an old resident there many times. During the war, a family with three sons serving in the Confederate forces occupied the house. The father, who had remained at home, was killed in the attic in 1863 by a roving band of bushwhackers. Soon after that tragic incident, Jacob ("Jake"), younger of the three brothers, deserted his regiment and came home. The plan was for his widowed mother and three sisters to hide him in the home until he could slip away far to the west. Another part of the scheme was to spread word that Jake had been killed and buried on some distant battlefield.

In a few days, virtually all of the residents in Bristol had heard the story of this tragic incident. It was then that word was sent out that a memorial service would be held for the son on a Sunday afternoon in the home. Of course, many sympathetic neighbors filled the three large rooms of the old house. Meanwhile, Jake had slipped under a huge low bed in the room adjoining the living room. He and one of his brothers had slept in the bed since their childhood. The bed had a large coverlet that reached the floor. He perceived that he would have a secure hiding place while he heard his own funeral preached. Perhaps what might be more satisfying to him would that he would be able to hear the mournful weeping of those friends and neighbors saddened by his tragic death.

As the time for the memorial service neared on that Sunday long ago, the house was filled, and all available chairs were taken. Two neighbors, Mrs. John N. (Lucinda) Bosang and Mrs. William H. (Lucy) Trammel, took seats side by side on the bed under which Jake was hiding. Both women were very opinionated and quick to defend whatever opinions might be held. Within a short time, they began discussing how old the dearly departed son was. That soon led into a heated argument. Mrs. Trammel knew that the boy was twenty-two, but Mrs. Bosang was equally sure that he was only *twenty* years old. Jake was hearing every word and well knew that both of them were wrong. Now he was one who was equally opinionated and pleasured in being correct. He could not stand hearing people making fools of themselves by strongly arguing something that he knew was wrong. The more he heard the more his Irish anger flared.

Finally, he reached the point to where his reason left him, and without foreseeing the consequences, he thrust his head out from under the bed right between the two women's feet. Glaring up at them, he yelled out, "You two old fools, you're both wrong! I'm just nineteen!" The result was horrendous! How would you feel if a boy, supposedly dead, stuck his head out from between your feet and began hollering things at you? Mrs. Trammel threw up both hands, screamed out, "Lord have mercy!" and fell back on the bed. Mrs. Bosang jumped up, squalled out like a wounded wildcat, tore from the room and went running through the adjoining living room, yelling, "Jake's ghost is right in that room under the bed!" Jake, realizing what he had done, rolled out, jumped up and went running wildly out of the room. That put him right behind Lucinda Bosang. Of course, that caused her to shift into overdrive, and her screams became wilder. Meanwhile, Jake, wanting those present to think he was from another dimension, began yelling out, "I'm a haint! I'm a haint!" That increased the tempo of an already wild stampede of the terrorized crowd, so much so that when he reached the front door, he found it tightly blocked. He whirled around and tore through the crowd in the kitchen, still loudly proclaiming that he was a "haint." Many just fainted away. Others leapt through the windows or doors.

One old woman, who my informant of long ago called "Ol' Aunt Hanner Lyle," jumped into the large kitchen fireplace and tried to get up the chimney. She could not manage the climb and just fainted away on the floor. One young man took refuge in a huge old wardrobe (as if a ghost couldn't go through wooden doors of a wardrobe). Alas, in the violent stampede of the panicked crowd, the wardrobe was turned over face forward. The young lad had considerable trouble kicking the back loose in order to escape.

Even the preacher, there to conduct the service, joined into the frenzied flight and ran into the kitchen. Finding all exits blocked, he ran up a narrow stairway into the attic. Alas, that was the same escape route taken by the "ghost." The preacher looked back and saw the supposedly dead Jake right behind. Luckily, there was a small attic window at the terrorized preacher's side. He rammed through it, taking sash and all, landed on the low back porch roof, jumped into the yard and ran up Washington Street, yelling as he went.

Jake, the supposed ghost, also jumped from the window onto the back porch. He fled southward and left the town. He was last seen going through Holston Valley, apparently heading for the mountains beyond. He was never seen or heard of again.

Although nothing further was heard of him, the memory of his final appearance lingered long on the minds of the people present that day.

PART III

BRISTOL TERRORS
AND TRAGEDIES

THE SINGING GHOST AT OLD ST. LUKE'S HOSPITAL

One unit of old St. Luke's Hospital still stands on the corner of Shelby and Tenth Streets in Bristol, Tennessee. It was originally a residence built as a speculative property by Uncle Will Smith, an early and noted contractor here. Uncle Will lived on Smith's Row within sight of this building.

The house was rather large for a residence, but the ample size of it is what made it useful as a hospital. After the hospital closed in 1925, the house again became a residence and, finally, a rooming house. Soon after it became a rooming house, a young man arrived in town and took a cheap room there that was high on the third floor. He was almost broke. For days, he desperately sought employment but without success. One morning, he went downtown to check out a lead on a job. It didn't work out. In fact, the prospective employer painted a dismal picture of the employment situation in Bristol. This was a crushing blow to the already despairing young man.

For the despondent and severely depressed individual, one rejection or one unpleasant incident can be the final push that puts one into the dark abyss of lost hope. This was apparently the case with this unfortunate young man. On his way back to the rooming house, he met a person who lived near there and with whom he had become lightly acquainted. This person later remembered that this fellow seemed unusually cheerful that

A ghostly singer has been heard in this remaining portion of St. Luke's Hospital. It has caused more than one occupant to move from the house.

morning and that there seemed to be a new spring in his step. This was so evident that this neighbor thought that perhaps this young man had found the employment he sought but made no mention of it. A last surge of peace and cheerfulness often comes to the despondent and despairing when they have finally given up resistance and fully surrendered to the idea that all hope is lost and that they must do what they strongly have an urge to do. To the trained observer, this is a serious danger sign— an indication that the depressed person who has long fought the urge of self-destruction now finds that such is not to be feared but to be a welcome way out.

This young man walked on to the rooming house, went straight up to his room and immediately hanged himself using a coat hanger as a noose. Those well versed in "ghostology" say that the site of a suicide is certain to be haunted. Supposedly, the miserable soul cannot leave the earth.

A few years ago, a young man from out of town bought this house. He did much to restore it and change it to a very livable family residence. The third-floor room where this tragedy occurred was made into a cozy, restful bedroom. One night, this new owner was walking along the third-floor hall singing a popular song of a time gone by. About the time he came even with the open door of the "suicide room," he came to the last line of that song, but his mind went blank. He simply could not remember the last line. Instantly, a strong but quivery male voice sounded in that room, singing the last line for him. The homeowner was shaken. He instantly entered the room and switched on the light. No one was there. The room was quiet and nothing was disturbed. Later, my friend, who likes to investigate ghostly "happenings," went up and stood near the haunted room. He started singing the same song and then paused. Immediately, a voice broke out in that room with the final line. Again there was no one there.

Others now own the house. I have heard that the room still has an eerie feeling but have not heard if the "singing ghost" has been singing again.

The Headless, Hungry Hobo

During the Great Depression, the Bristol railroad yards became "infested," as one old-timer put it, with hobos seeking the opportunity to hop a freight train for a ride to somewhere, most of them knew not where. They just believed that life would be better if they could go to some distant location.

Upper Spencer Street (now known as Martin Luther King Boulevard) was then lined with humble cottages facing the railroad yards. These homes, as unpromising as they were, became prime targets for hobos seeking handouts. In one of those houses lived a young widow with three small children. She was barely able to provide food for her family.

Late one afternoon there was a knock at her door. When opened, she found a rather tall, rough-featured man who was poorly dressed in dirty and worn clothing, except for a clean white shirt that stood out in contrast to the other shabby clothes he wore. Likely it had been given to him from a home at which he begged. He was extremely weak, as his request for food was moaned out rather than spoken clearly. He told her that he was hungry and wanted food badly. Sadly, she had to turn him away, as there was no food to spare.

During that night, she couldn't help but wonder if he had found food. She had a great sympathy for all needy persons, but there was simply nothing she could do. Some time during that night, there was a gruesome accident in the railroad yards.

Again, early the next morning, there was a knock at her kitchen door. She opened the door. There stood the hungry hobo, but what a change! He still wore the white shirt, but it was now soaked with blood, and he had no head! He was carrying his head by its long bushy hair in his right hand. From that bodiless head came the mournful plea, "Oh, I'm hungry, so hungry." She barely heard those words, for she fainted and fell backward in the kitchen floor. Finally, when she came to, she awoke the children and fled to her parents' home near Mumpower Park. There she learned that the hobo had been found dead in the railroad yard. Evidently, he had tried to jump on a train that was moving too fast. He was thrown under the wheels, and his head had been completely severed from his body.

This young woman soon remembered that she had left her children's warm nightclothes at home and knew that they would definitely need them sleeping in an unheated room in her father's house. She took her father with her and went back home for the needed clothes. They started home just as dusk was falling over the town. As they neared the Columbia Street railroad underpass, they suddenly heard a moaning, groaning voice right behind them saying, "Oh, I'm so hungry, so hungry." Both whirled around, and there, behind them and coming closer, was the headless, hungry hobo, still carrying his head in his hand—and that severed head was speaking. Both she and her father shot through that underpass with the headless ghost in hot pursuit. Neighbors saw them sprinting up Columbia Street, but none of them saw the ghost. When they ran through the home gate, that horrible ghost simply vanished.

There was not much sleep in that home through the long night. The widow had been shaken so deeply that she never went home again. A bachelor from Kingtown had been trying to persuade her to marry him. You might say that the ghost played Cupid, for rather than go home she agreed to marry this man and soon moved to his home in Kingtown. In all my writing of ghost stories, I think this is the first ghost tale that I've heard wherein the ghost played matchmaker, but it was true in this case. She was again a widow when I came to Bristol and was one of the first

The entrance to the Columbia Avenue underpass looks foreboding at best—more so when one knows that a headless hobo is sometimes encountered there.

people to apply for aid when I began my welfare work here. She later told me this story and said that she was still reluctant to answer a knock at her door.

Now what of the future of the headless, hungry hobo ghost? The next spring following the death of this hobo, two young boys were fishing in Beaver Creek just a short distance below the Columbia Street underpass. Suddenly, they heard a moaning voice behind them saying, "Oh, I'm hungry, oh so hungry." They quickly looked around, and there stood a man with no head—at least not a head in the right place. He was carrying it by the hair in his right hand, and that head was speaking to them. Well, the boys left all their equipment behind and split that creek wide open as they raced through the railroad yards and on to their homes on Spencer Street. In the fall of 1934, the headless, hungry hobo appeared again one foggy morning at the back door of the former widow's house on Spencer Street where he begged shortly before he was killed. It was occupied by others, but not for long—they left the house the same day.

On through the following years, others have reported seeing the ghostly sight of this headless man, including some who were riding passenger trains through the yards and told of seeing this horrible sight as the train moved slowly out of the yards. In 1992, a man reported to me that he was jogging through the underpass one night about ten o'clock. He heard someone running right behind him. Looking back, he saw, in the dim light, the headless ghost. He froze in fear for a moment, but on this occasion that horrible ghost added a little more to the show. He threw his head, and it rolled right between my jogger friend's feet. Well that jogger unfroze instantly and started a dead sprint racing toward home, loudly yelling each step.

I have had no reports lately of this headless, hungry hobo ghost. I do know that many people who walk for exercise dread walking through that underpass at Columbia Street because of a fear based on the stories surrounding this ghost. At best, this underpass is a scary place, even in daytime. I sometimes drive through it but have never encountered the man carrying his own head.

THE HAUNTED PILLOW

Of all the places to be haunted, the bed and bedroom are two places where you do not wish to have ghosts appear. How can you sleep well if you know that a ghost has been in the room? In this story, there was no ghostly appearance, only ghostly sounds, but perhaps sounds are just as frightening as appearances.

One early Saturday morning several years ago, a man living on Mary Street in Bristol, Virginia, drove out to make the rounds of several early spring yard sales. Pickings are usually pretty good at such times, but this particular event was the most unforgettable yard sale and purchase he had ever made. He got two pillows for only fifty cents. He and his wife had badly needed them, for they had just put up a bed in what had been the junk room. Furnishings for that bed had been a little short. He took the pillows and instead of going to the other sales, immediately returned home to share the good news with his wife. She was very pleased with the purchase of such a fine, clean, plump set of pillows for such a bargain— so pleased that she replaced the set on their own bed with these far superior examples he had just brought in. The original set was relegated to the second bedroom. Both were eagerly anticipating bedtime, when they could try out the husband's most fortunate purchase.

The haunted pillow ghost once terrorized a couple living in this apartment house on Moore Street in Bristol, Virginia.

That night, the husband, enjoying the comfort of his new pillow, soon drifted to a pleasant and restful sleep. A little after midnight, he was slowly awakened by what sounded like the screams of a woman. He arose and went to a window to listen, thinking that the sounds of distress were coming from somewhere down the street. After opening the window and intently listening, no sound could be heard. Thinking that he may have been dreaming, he went back to bed and soon drifted off to sleep. It happened again, and he arose from his bed and went to the window and then to the porch. Still, nothing could be heard. Returning to his bed, he lay awake for a while and, turning to his left side (his favorite sleeping position), immediately heard the same sound again. Like the faint sounds of a radio playing in a distant room, he heard the terrified and agonized screams of a woman. He rose up and there was no sound. Pressing his ear to the pillow, the screams were heard again, faintly but there no doubt. A bit terrified, he set bolt upright in bed.

By then his wife was awake. After he explained the situation to her, she, a bit irritated for having been awakened from a deep sleep, snapped back, "Oh, you 'fraidy cat. Give me that pillow. I'm not afraid to sleep on it." The swap was made. In a few minutes, she was almost asleep again when suddenly she jerked awake. She, too, had heard the screams in the pillow. Right then another swap was made. Those bargain pillows were put on the backroom bed. The old set was brought to their bed again. There was little sleep for that puzzled, nervous couple for the rest of the night.

The next morning, this man went to his aged grandmother's house a few blocks away. This grandmother, a gnarled old woman from the most remote area of Scott County, Virginia, quickly made her analysis of the situation. "Why son, I bound you thay's some awful thing that happened around that pillow," she confidently replied. "Maybe somebody was murdered on it or just died on it." The curious grandson lost no time in going back to the house where the purchase had been made, but the family members there, making a final cleanup, were very grim and tight-lipped and would tell them nothing.

A little later, he went to the lady who lived next door to where the sale had been made. There, he was told the whole story. A young couple had lived in the house along with a sister of the wife. The husband had been a habitual drinker. Late one night, he came home from a round with his drinking buddies. He was more or less in a drunken stupor. His angry wife arose from her bed and chided him about this, causing a violent argument to ensue. According to her sister, who was in an adjoining room, the enraged husband went into the kitchen and slammed the door behind him. The wife returned to her bed. After a few minutes, she arose and went to the kitchen. Strangely, she found it dark. When she switched on the light, she was greeted by a ghastly scene. The husband was slumped over the table, which was covered in blood. He had taken a sharp butcher knife and slashed his throat from ear to ear. The sister further told that the wife ran screaming to her bed, jumped in and grabbed her pillow, using it to muffle her agonizing screams. The sister, not knowing the horror, ran to the kitchen but fainted straight away after seeing such an awful sight. When she came to, her sister was dead. Evidently, in her terror, she had held that pillow so tight that she had smothered herself to death.

The neighbor went on to tell that she had seen the contents of the house sold in a yard sale recently. If there was a pillow sold, she was sure she would never have bought it. As a matter of fact, she had not even gone over to check for bargains. Before the man had even left her front porch stoop, he had fully decided that he would not have that pillow either, or the other "silent" one for that matter. He went home straightaway and supposed that stuffing them in the garbage can was a bad idea, perhaps for fear that screams might begin coming from there. Instead, he waited until after dark, walked down the street and across the Mary Street Bridge and dropped them on the tracks below. His old pillow may have not been comfortable, but at least it wasn't haunted.

Ghosts in the Storm

It happened some time during the Depression years. The month was June, and those who told me the story years ago thought it was during the end of that month. Whenever it was, it was one of those sultry, muggy late spring days that are just right for severe thunderstorms. One did strike Bristol about 4:00 p.m. Clouds that had gathered in the west turned darker and darker, finally becoming a deep, inky green that nearly always signaled an approaching violent storm. Thunder began to roll, and lightning flashed from cloud to earth, the most dangerous kind. Those flashes became near constant as the storm rolled into west Bristol with gusts of tree-bending wind.

Far out on Broad Street lived a family whose young son, wife and new baby lived next door. This son's house was small and not too well built. As the fury of the violent storm increased, that little house began to creak, rock and tremble. The very frightened young mother grabbed the baby and tried to make a run for the family home next door. As she ran near a large tree, a bolt of lightning struck and tore that tree asunder, instantly killing both mother and child. The family soon sold the home and, along with the widowed son, moved away.

Before long, the house was sold to another family. Sometime after this family moved in, there came another sultry afternoon when a violent storm moved into the western part of the city. During the height of that storm, the couple, watching intently from the living room window, suddenly saw a young woman with a baby in her arms running across the yard. They, knowing that no one was living next door, assumed this woman had been walking in the street and had been caught in the raging storm. They both ran out the front door to help her in, but when that mother and child reached a certain point in the yard, *whoosh*—they just vanished. Even in later years, there have been reports of the mother and baby running across the yard during the height of a storm.

One of the first cases I handled in my welfare work here involved a young couple who lived in the little house that had been occupied by the unfortunate mother and child. They said that not only had they seen the mother and child in the yard during stormy times, but they also had seen other ghostly manifestations in and around their little house. Sometimes they would hear a baby crying in the middle of the night, the sound seemingly coming from the adjoining bedroom. If they went into that room, the sound would move into another room and so on through the house. There had also been several times when they were awakened by a piercing scream seemingly coming from the yard outside their bedroom window. No one else in the area could hear the screams. I think this couple was much relieved when I managed to find them a modest cottage on Sullins Street, a home that was supposedly "ghost free."

The last report that I had of the "storm ghost" was in 2002. Beware, though, you who live in that area, when storm clouds roll in from the west.

LOVERS IN LIFE, LOVERS IN DEATH

Milton Webber came to Bristol, Virginia, from Arkansas (perhaps Batesville, Independence County) at about the age of twenty-five. Apparently he was somewhat of a drifter but managed to get a job with Buffman Mills. He secured room and board with an old lady on East Main (now State) Street and appeared to be settling down. He was a handsome man and became very well liked by those who knew him. His landlady had a girl, Sally Haddon, employed to work around the boardinghouse. The girl cleaned rooms, made beds, helped in the kitchen and served at mealtime. She was only fifteen but rather precocious and a very efficient worker.

Now Milton Webber got his eye on the girl and soon tried to start a courtship. The girl was very willing, but her father, a rather stern and suspicious sort of fellow, expressly forbade the girl even so much as to be friendly with any of the male boarders. So what courting the couple was able to do had to be very much on the sly.

This man killed his daughter and her husband and then went insane. The two he killed are still said to haunt East Hill Cemetery.

Sly and infrequent it may have been, but it certainly was effective! Within a few weeks, Milton had persuaded the young girl to marry him. He rented a small house on upper Williams Street for their new home. By lying about the girl's age, a license was obtained and a time secretly set. The girl finished her work after dark one night and then met Milton down by what is now the First Baptist Church. From there, they walked to the home of Reverend A.H. Burrough (the marrying parson) at 117 Third Street. Reverend Burrough married the couple, and then, hand in hand, they walked to their new home on upper Williams Street.

Of course, when Sally did not return home, the father started to search for her. At the boardinghouse, he was told that the girl had married, and it was thought she was going to live somewhere in town, the exact location being unknown. The father vowed, then and there, that he would find the couple and, when he did, that he would kill the young husband.

For the next couple of weeks, the angry father searched all over town, but without success. Finally, he learned that Milton worked at Buffman Mills. He immediately went there but was told that Milton had quit his job a week or so before. He was then working for McCrary Brothers Construction Company, but the father was unaware of this.

One day—my informant from long ago thought it was on a Saturday afternoon—Mr. Haddon, still seething with anger, went to a hillside considered to be "no man's land" just behind the intersection of Williams Street. There he planned to cut wood for his cookstove. While chopping wood there, he looked up and was startled to see his daughter and new husband emerge from a little cottage that stood directly across the street from where he was working. He dropped his axe and, with pistol in hand, charged down the hill toward the unsuspecting couple. He had reached the street when the couple saw him. By then, he had his pistol raised, aiming it at Milton. Sally saw this and quickly jumped in front of her husband just as the first shot fired. That shot hit her in the throat. She fell to the ground, strangling in her own blood, soon to die there in the street. Milton took three shots in the chest, one of them piercing his heart. He died instantly.

The father was apprehended and taken to the local jail. Within two or three hours, he went stark raving mad. He began to try to kill himself by ramming his head against the jail wall, all the while screaming out that Sally was just before him in each place he turned. He was bound with ropes but continued to rave on until he suddenly died just before midnight.

Young Milton Webber was buried in the lower part of what became the pauper's section of East Hill Cemetery. Sally was buried farther up the hill near the present western driveway of what is now Hugh Hagan Drive of the same cemetery. My informant from long ago had forgotten where the father who died near midnight was buried but knew that they were not buried in the same lot.

The night after the burial, an old couple who lived on upper Williams Street just a short distance above where Milton and Sally had lived were sitting on their front porch just as darkness settled over the town. Their house was located just across the street from that section of the cemetery where the slain couple had been buried recently. About 9:00 p.m., the old couple arose from their chairs to go inside to retire. Before they entered their front door, they saw a shimmering yellow light slowly rising up from

Milton's newly made grave. At the same time, a similar light was seen rising up from Sally's grave. The latter light stayed there, while the one from Milton's grave slowly made its way up the hill. When the ghostly lights came together, they became one and disappeared. All was dark again in East Hill Cemetery.

Over the following years, those strange lights were seen several times by various people. Old-timers of the town called them the "ghost-courting lights." An old black lady, still living at the time of this writing, once told me that when her family lived within sight of that part of the cemetery, they would sit on the front porch and watch for those lights. If they appeared, her father would jokingly say, "Well, there goes Milton to go see Miss Sally."

There have been reports of the "courting lights" within recent years. A few years ago, a police officer was driving up Williams Street about 2:00 a.m. All seemed to be quiet and well in that neighborhood. Out of the corner of his eye, the officer saw two lights flare up in the cemetery. Suspecting that vandals were at work (there had been some vandalism there at the time), he raced to the Williams Street entry and over to the driveway near the burial sites. The lights were still showing as he neared that section but then suddenly disappeared. He turned his spotlight right on the area where the lights had been, but nothing seemed to indicate the presence of anyone or anything. Had he witnessed a reappearance of the ghostly courting lights? Perhaps he had.

Note: An old resident of that section of Bristol, who was somewhat of an amateur poet, became inspired and wrote what became a locally well-known ballad about this event. He called it "Lovers in Life, Lovers in Death." It was still being played and sung, albeit rarely, when this author came to Bristol some fifty years ago.

THE HAUNTED GEORGIA AVENUE BRIDGE

Daily, a lot of people pass over the little bridge on Georgia Avenue near the former Cortrim location in Bristol, Tennessee. Most of them do not know that many Bristolians say that this bridge is haunted. A man recently told me that he once had what he called "a real live encounter with a ghost" at that bridge.

The story goes that many years ago, a mother with a baby was driving across another bridge some distance upstream. Her car ran off the bridge into the flooding stream. The mother was spared, but the baby was drowned. The body was washed downstream and lodged against the Georgia Avenue Bridge. The mother, in profound grief, soon pined away and died. Soon afterward, her ghost began to appear near the bridge. Several have reported seeing her there.

My friend who told me this said that one night when he was a boy, he was playing outside and hid from his playmate near this bridge. Shortly, he was startled to see a light coming slowly down the stream. As it neared, he saw that it was a woman dressed in white carrying a lantern in her hand. She was walking in the stream. Within twenty feet of him, she disappeared. All was dark again. He had no doubt seen the ghost of the mother hunting for her baby.

Another story that involves the Georgia Avenue Bridge concerns a wrecked car that leaves no wreckage. This ghost usually appears in broad daylight.

People living in the area have reported seeing a jet-black car coming down the slope from toward Paperville Road. When near the bridge, the car suddenly leaves the road and plunges over the abutment down

The Georgia Avenue Bridge occasionally plays host to a pair of very unusual ghosts.

into the stream at the bridge. Time and again people—including my friend who told me the story of the mother hunting her baby there— would hasten to the scene to find nothing. There would be no wreckage. The car would have just vanished. There is no evidence to ever indicate an accident at all. There is no known cause for this ghost, nor has ever anyone been able to explain why such a thing happens.

The Distraught Ghost

The night was completely clear. Not a cloud was in sight. A bright moon was just rising over the eastern horizon. A man driving along Randall Street Expressway (now Martin Luther King Boulevard) was about even with the west door of the depot when what appeared to be a dazzling bolt of lightning cracked down directly in front of his car. Lightning from a cloudless sky? That is what it appeared to be—but it wasn't. What he saw was a ghost that has appeared from time to time for well over 125 years. It all goes back to a tragedy that occurred at that point in March 1875.

A large hotel known as the Virginia House stood on old Front Street across from the depot. At that time, there were no dining cars on trains. On certain schedules, trains had dining stops in Bristol. Passengers could go to the Virginia House for a quick meal. To make it convenient for those passengers, John G. Wood, who then operated the hotel, had a bridge built from the depot over the street to his establishment. It entered in on the second floor. This bridge was built mainly so passengers could avoid the often very muddy street.

In those days, the hotel not only kept overnight guests but also had rooms that could be rented for regular boarders. Among them was a railroad brakeman. While living at the Virginia House, he fell in love with a Bristol girl. They planned a mid-spring wedding. In late March, he returned from a regular run to find that this girl had eloped! The poor brakeman skipped supper that night and, in a very dark, depressed state, went silently up to his room. A cook, coming to work the next morning, bumped into his feet as she walked under that bridge. Sometime during the night, the distraught man had hanged himself from the rail of that bridge.

Ever since that sad event, there have been times when a flash of light is seen at the point where the old bridge crossed the street.

Ghosts in the Knobs

The knobs that somewhat divide large portions of Bristol form an unknown land to many who live here. I know of many Bristolians who have been born, lived and died here yet were never on even the lower slopes of those knobby hills. To some they are fascinating. To others they are a bit mysterious, even fearful. Certainly they present a puzzling maze of hills and valleys in which one could easily get lost. This has happened on numerous occasions. And yes, they are ghosts in those hills. There are a few burial sites in the knobs. They are small family plots. Those of which I have knowledge contain no more than five graves.

Far back, a family lived in a cabin atop one of those many narrow ridges that mark the area. I have been told that the father and two grown sons in this family died in quick succession. They were buried a little farther up the ridge from where their cabin stood. Late in the afternoon, after the last of the three were buried, the widow and her mother just closed the cabin door, walked out of the knobs, passed through downtown Bristol near nightfall and simply disappeared. No one ever knew what happened to them. The old cabin eventually rotted down. A few old foundation stones and chimney rocks may remain at the site. The graves are now lost in underbrush and covered with many autumns of fallen leaves. Those men have been long gone, but they keep appearing now and then. But, certainly, in a distinct and altered form.

Not long after I came to Bristol, three youths went exploring in the knobs one balmy October Sunday afternoon. As they went from valley to valley, they slowly became aware that they were lost. Of course they were frightened and desperately commenced trying to find their way out. Suddenly, they heard a "clacking" sound just behind the bushes. They looked, and all of a sudden, a walking skeleton popped up out of those bushes! The boys "popped" forward in extra high gear. But, right in their path, another skeleton appeared. They immediately whirled around, but another appeared right in front of them. The last remaining direction lay open, and fortunately no skeleton blocked the path. The boys ran northward and shortly found themselves at the rim of high ridge looking down on Windsor Avenue. They were lost no more.

Did those ghostly skeletons direct those "lost boys" out of the woods? Many who have heard this story believe so. The boys' aged grandmother later told me that guardian angels can appear in many forms. If a guardian angel ever appears to me, I hope the standard form will be used.

BRISTOL'S STRANGEST GHOST

It happened about 1903, soon after the new Bristol depot was constructed. A local lady and her six-year-old son were waiting on the station platform for the arrival of the morning train from the east. The husband/father had been away for several days and was scheduled to arrive on that train. Suddenly, the little boy gleefully called out, "Mama, Mama, look up there! A cat's coming yonder!" Sure enough, on the platform something white was swiftly moving toward them. It appeared to have a dark spot on top of its head. That little boy just loved cats, so he ran down the platform to meet it, eagerly anticipating the joy of petting the kitty.

Bristol's strangest ghost once appeared at the Bristol Depot. Several other ghosts are said to haunt this 108-year-old structure.

The mother's attention was drawn in another direction momentarily. However, when the little boy came running back, excitedly calling out, "It's not a cat, Mama, it's a foot!" she quickly did a double take. Indeed, it was a bare foot with no body attached, just skipping along the platform. It was deathly white and all bloody at the top, as if recently severed. That bloody top was what looked like a spot on the "kitty's" head. Well, there were soon other feet skipping—"running" would be a better word—along the platform, through the depot and across the street as the woman, almost dragging her little boy, fled in terror.

It was such a strange happening, the woman was afraid to tell it, lest she be called "insane." A bit later, when others had the same experience and told it, she became bolder and told her story. Locals who were well versed in "ghostology" allowed that it was the ghost foot of a workman whose real foot had been severed in the railroad yards months before. They said it was "still hunting its owner." The real foot had been buried in East Hill Cemetery. A local psychic declared that the ghost foot would never rest until the owner of that foot died and was buried near it. Strangely, the owner did die later that year. He was buried up there near his severed foot, and that strangest of all Bristol ghosts was never seen at the local depot again.

PART IV
MESSAGES FROM THE GRAVE

ANSWERING SERVICE

Did you ever have a ghost answer your telephone or get a ghost when you called someone? Not likely, but just a few years ago, something like this did happen in a Bristol, Tennessee home.

In this particular Bristol household, the retired husband's favorite domain was a comfortable den downstairs. There he read or watched television just about all day long. The wife, who was not much of a television fan or a reader, spent much of her time in an upstairs sewing room. There she spent hours in knitting, crocheting or piecing quilts. Both rooms were equipped with telephones. At a ring, both husband and wife usually answered. Then, when it was determined for whom the call was intended, the other would hang up.

After several years of retirement, the husband's health became bad, but he continued to sit or lie down in the den for much of his waking time. One day, while in the midst of a telephone conversation, he suddenly died. His body was discovered when his wife came down to announce supper. The telephone was still clutched in his lifeless hand.

The widow lived on at the home place for a few years after. On the first anniversary of her late husband's death, the still sad widow was sitting alone in the sewing room doing a bit of crochet work when the telephone rang. She was slow in reaching for the phone. As she did so, the phone suddenly stopped ringing. That used to happen a lot when her husband picked up the phone downstairs. It puzzled her that this had happened after only two or three rings. Usually there were more. When she lifted the receiver and placed it to her ear to check, the unmistakable voice of her husband was heard conversing with Regina Halstead, an old friend of hers from her college days. She had not been in touch with her for several years. Then she heard the voice say, "Oh yes, I am very well but I think I hear Beatrice [the widow's name]." And then the voice called up to her, "Oh, Beatrice, are you there? It's Regina, she wants to talk with you." It all sounded so familiar, so much so that for a few seconds the widow forgot the situation. "Yes, I am here," she began, and then, "Oh my Gosh" she said, when she realized she had just heard her dead husband's voice on the phone. She screamed and tore out of the room, bounced down the stairs and fled out the front door. She leapt across the back lawn and burst through the neighbor's front door without bothering to knock or ring the bell. After she was able to get her breath and blurt out her strange tale of woe, the neighbor called the police, thinking that a prankster was in the widow's house pulling a cruel trick on her. The police came and made a diligent search, but there was nothing to indicate that anyone else had been in the house.

After that harrowing experience, this lady would never spend another night or day there. She sold the house and contents and moved into a furnished apartment. She would never have a telephone installed in her new quarters. This likely contributed to her demise. For there, alone one night, she suffered a heart attack and, unable to call for help, she died.

A NOTE FROM BEYOND

About 1939, a young Bristol widow did well when she married a middle-aged bachelor who was a local businessman. He moved her and her two children into his nice and commodious home on Windsor Avenue (at that time, Windsor Avenue was a very stately address). He proved to be a kind, loving and provident husband and became a very good stepfather to the two young children. After two or three years of marriage, they had a child of their own.

In the home, a large notepad was kept near the back door on which the two exchanged notes when necessary. One afternoon, the wife was

Pictured here is the husband who, after his death, wrote a message that proved beneficial to his widow.

away visiting her mother. After returning home, she found a note from her husband on the large pad. It stated that he had to make a business trip to Kingsport and would not be home for supper but would be in late that night. She and the children went on to bed at their usual time.

Near midnight, she was awakened by a loud knock on her front door. She thought this to be strange because her husband had his own key. When she arose and peered cautiously through the front glass, she saw a policeman standing there. He had come to tell her that her husband had been killed in a car accident on "Suicide Curve," as the locals call it, a short distance west of Blountville, Tennessee.

About a week after her husband was buried, the yet grieving widow had a sleepless night. About 2:00 a.m., she was startled when she saw a light come on in the kitchen. She arose and upon investigation found that it was the light over the little table where the large notepad was kept. She well knew that the top page had been left clear, but she readily saw that there was then writing on it. Upon closer examination, she was shocked to find that the writing was that of her deceased husband. In that "note from beyond," he told her that an old wardrobe in an unused bedroom of the large house had a false bottom and went on to instruct her how to remove it (the wife had never liked that old wardrobe and actually had planned to soon give it to the local Salvation Army).

Very shaken by all of this, she lost no time calling her brother, who lived a short distance away. He came, followed the instructions given in this ghostly note and found the false bottom. In the cavity below this false bottom were numerous bundles of $100 bills. The hidden treasure amounted to more than $100,000. The ghost of her kind husband had done her a great favor from beyond. She was a good steward over this find and the rest of the assets he left her, and she was able to live comfortably for the rest of her life.

THE GHOSTLY GREETER

Bristol is a city of churches. They range from very large to very small and all sizes in between. This ghostly manifestation I write about here happened in a church that was very small at the time but has grown to be one of the largest in the city. I had become a close friend of the pastor of this small church—he had been taking instruction in the same night school that I was attending at the time. He told me this story in strictest confidence (about 1955), asking me never to reveal it during his lifetime. He feared that if the news got out, it might create a stigma on his ministry. He also feared that if the story were told, it might hurt the progress of the church. But as happens often, I heard the same story from several different persons thinking they were the only person who knew it. That's the way secrecy goes, you know. I think that helped to prove what Benjamin Franklin said: "Two people may keep a secret if one of them be dead."

In this church was a man who was almost ninety years old. He was much loved and highly respected by his fellow church members. He lived within a few blocks of the church and always insisted on walking to and from the services. He said it "fired him up" for the day. He always arrived early and took his place at the front door to greet the members as they arrived. To him, each service was a family reunion. He would warmly clasp the hand of each person and cheerfully say, "I am so happy, dear sister/brother, and am so glad that you are in the Lord's family." Finally, the old brother, after reaching the age of ninety-five, died. His funeral was held in the little church he loved so well. He was buried late that same day in the Susong Cemetery that was not far from this church. The funeral was held on a Wednesday, and a prayer meeting was to be held that night. The young pastor went to the church a bit early to turn the lights on as the deceased brother had always done. It was winter and darkness fell early. He unlocked the door and reached for the light switch when suddenly, from within the darkness, an icy-cold hand firmly clasped his. Then, a quivering, shaky voice, seeming to come from far away, gave the familiar greeting: "I'm so happy to see you, dear brother, and I am so glad that you are in the family of the Lord."

Well, that young pastor may have been in the family of the Lord, but he sure wasn't glad to be in the presence of a ghost. In stark terror, he tried hard to pull away and jerked time and again, but the cold, bony hand held firm. Slowly but steadily, he felt himself being pulled into the dark church and down the aisle into the pulpit. With his free hand he tried to grab the end of a pew. Then he tried to call out but could not. His blood turned to ice, his hair stood on end, but still the ghost pulled on for what seemed like an eternity. Then, the lights came on of their own accord, and there was nothing there but himself—and as he expressed it, the lights revealed a very frightened man.

Well, as the members came in later that night, most easily noticed that the pastor wasn't himself. He was very pale with a distinct tremor in his voice. At the close of an unusually short service, he excused himself, leaving others to close up the church, uncharacteristic for the pastor. He resigned the following Sunday. Forty years later, when he was on his deathbed in a hospital in Kingsport, Tennessee, I visited him and sat long by his bedside. He could still talk, and we talked about this ghostly happening so many years before. He said he thought of this ghostly incident nearly every day since and that he still was hesitant to reach into a dark room for a light switch. He died that night. You know, it made an impression on me that a man so near death still maintained the original story he had told me of that ghost in that little church. What can you make of that? Would not most people be frightened into honesty if they knew they were about to die? I will let every reader form his own opinion. And no longer bound by my promise, I am telling you this story as he told it to me.

I'LL BE HOME TOMORROW NIGHT

Dr. Alfred Moore Carter came to Bristol from Elizabethton, Carter County, Tennessee, soon after the Civil War. He then set up his medical practice, with his first office being located within the old James King home on the northeast corner of Main (State) and Moore Streets. He was quickly accepted by the fast-developing town and soon had a thriving and effective practice here.

The owner of the old King home at that time was Charlotte (Chassie) King, a daughter of Cyrus King and a granddaughter of the original owner of her home. In a couple years or so, Dr. Carter and Chassie were married. Three children soon came to brighten the Carter home. Then tragedy struck. Two of the children died within a short time, followed a little later by the mother. This left Dr. Carter alone with one surviving child, little Maude Carter (who later became the wife of Ellis K. Crymble). Dr. Carter remained a widower for a short time and then married Miss Nannie Zimmerman, a daughter of Bristol's first doctor, B.F. Zimmerman. In the mid-1880s, the Carters bought a house on Fifth Street. This house was then almost new, having been erected in 1881 by James P. Lewis for Archibald Pickens, a local jeweler. The Carters occupied the house for many years. Indeed, it served as home to Mrs. Carter through her widowed years, until her death in 1936. One was afforded wonderful views as it overlooked beautiful Anderson Park. In later years, it was painted pink, and most Bristolians referred to it as the "Pink House." It was demolished a few years ago.

Soon after the move was made to Fifth Street, Dr. Carter developed the habit of taking early evening walks over the neighborhood. His usual route was to go down Fifth Street to Shelby, then west on Shelby to Sixth, then south on Sixth to Anderson and then down Anderson to Fifth Street and home. This he did with such regularity that folks living along the route could just about set their watches and clocks by his regular passage

Dr. A.M. Carter, a prominent businessman and Bristol physician, appeared in Bristol as a ghost on the day he died.

of their homes. In later years, the Carters began spending winters in central Florida, but the very day they came home, usually in late April or very early May, Dr. Carter would resume his evening walks.

In mid-April 1915, the weather in the Bristol area became unseasonably warm, so warm that folks were able to sit comfortably on their front porches even during the evening hours. One evening a family, then occupying a house near Sixth and Anderson, had gone out after the evening meal to sit on their spacious front porch. Soon after they sat down, their little dog ran down the front walk and continued a short distance down the street barking loudly. This was no surprise, as the little dog did so each day, apparently stirred up by Dr. Carter's walking by. The family often spoke of how Dr. Carter's coming was announced by their little dog. Sure enough they looked, and along the street came the tall, dark figure of the well-known Bristol doctor. As usual, he had a cane swinging on his arm (he seldom touched the ground with it), and of course, there was the ever-present derby hat he always wore at a certain angle on his head. As he neared the gate, the head of that family called out, "Why Dr. Carter, how nice it is to see you. You're home early this year!" Strangely, the doctor replied, "No, I'll be home tomorrow night." Usually he would have stopped and chatted for a while. This strange answer and action left the family very puzzled.

By telephone later that night, they learned the doubly shocking news. Dr. Carter had suddenly died the day before! His body would arrive by train (Train No. 42) the following evening. Sleep was a bit difficult for that family. The shock of his death was distressing, and that, coupled with what had apparently been a ghostly appearance, was not conducive to tranquil rest. That family, along with a large crowd of other Bristolians, was at the depot the following evening when old 42 sounded the mournful wail as it steamed into the local depot. As the casket was slowly taken from the baggage car, the family remembered those words: "I'll be home tomorrow night."

Dr. Carter had indeed come home, but this time he was here to stay.

PART V

HAUNTED HOMES

THE QUAIL RUN GHOST

Quail Run is a well-named street running off Vance Drive near Rooster Front Park in Bristol, Tennessee. In the early 1800s, the large and well-maintained John O'Brian farm sprawled around this picturesque location. Soon after the O'Brians moved there, they selected a spot back near the hill line for a family cemetery. It was at the upper edge of the cleared fields and pastures. That area of the cemetery is now overgrown with brush and trees. No markers or even fieldstone markers could be found there when I first visited the site more than fifty years ago. Evidently, over the years they have fallen down and have been covered with dirt or have been carried away. I might explain here that John O'Brian's wife was a half-sister to Colonel James King's wife, who lived just below there at the mouth of Steele's Creek at Holly Bend Plantation. It was here that Mrs. O'Brian was sitting conversing with her sister by the fireplace when death overcame Mrs. King in 1806. She is buried in what is now known as Ordway Cemetery.

The first member of the family to be buried in the O'Brian family lot was little Johnny O'Brian, age four, who died in 1803 of typhoid. One night, soon after this child was buried, a small group of neighborhood boys went up in the knobs hunting. It was about midnight when they came down from the knobs. Their path lay right by the O'Brian cemetery. Coming near it, they were greatly startled and badly frightened to see a

This young man once fled from the ghost at the O'Brian Cemetery on Quail Run.

dim light moving slowly around the newly made grave. Then came the distinct sound of a child crying. How long this went on the boys did not know. They were not there long but rather fled quickly to the O'Brian home, where their fearful tale was told. John O'Brian and a brother who lived there quickly arose from bed and hastened to the cemetery, thinking that a child may be lost and wandering around up there. Nothing was found. All was quiet and still.

In time, a public trail was established leading from Beaver Creek over to a cluster of two or three cabins in those knobs. This trail followed the approximate route of present Quail Run and thus passed near the O'Brian family cemetery. One night, a youth was out very late and was returning to his home in the knobs. The moon was full and the sky was clear. It was one of those nights that old-timers would describe as being "bright as day." This youth knew about the cemetery and later admitted that he was a bit nervous. He hurried along, trying not to look toward the cemetery. But out of the corner of his eye he saw something white slowly circling around little Johnny's grave. He described that "something" as being about the size of a turkey gobbler. Then the sound of a child crying drifted mournfully out of the little cemetery. If anything else was to be seen or heard, the lad never knew it. In long leaps, he went over the hills and reached his home in record time. Over the following years, others told of seeing or hearing strange things in or near that lonely burial ground.

Two more of the O'Brian children soon died, followed by a nearly grown daughter. Then John O'Brian was carried there to rest with his children. Several years later, the aged mother, Martha Goodson O'Brian, rested among her own. Soon after Mrs. O'Brian was buried, a neighbor living across Beaver Creek sat on her porch one night, still in grief over the loss of her much-loved neighbor. As she sadly sat, looking through the moon-bathed night and then over to the old cemetery on the hill, she became aware of a dim light that seemed to be getting brighter. Then that light shot upward and disappeared in the sky, leaving all silent and as dark as before. Actually, this viewing of what appeared to be something ghostly was of great comfort to this woman, for she thought it meant that the spirit of her neighbor had gone to the realms above.

In October 1902, a man was gathering corn in a field near this little cemetery. It was one of those mild, blue-skied October days without a cloud in sight. Suddenly, what appeared to be a streak of cloud-to-earth lightning cracked downward into the jungle-like area where the O'Brian cemetery was located, instantly followed by an earth-jarring sound of thunder. Large billowy smoke clouds then filled the thicket and rolled upward, but no fire could be seen. Stunned and somewhat frightened, the man left the field and hastened to his home on the banks of Beaver Creek. His home stood on the site of the O'Brian house. His wife and children there had heard nothing. He inquired of nearby neighbors, but they had not heard a thing either. He then was certain that this must have been a ghostly manifestation. It was told that this tenant farmer moved away the very next day, leaving his ungathered corn in the field.

Throughout the years, stories have been told of ghostly happenings in the vicinity of that old cemetery. Some report having seen moving lights nearly always accompanied by the sounds of a crying child.

Today, there are many fine homes located very near this deserted, overgrown and very nearly lost two-hundred-year-old burying ground. It is doubtful if any Bristolians who occupy those homes know of the cemetery or the ghostly happenings there. But who knows? On some dark night the ghost of the O'Brian cemetery may appear again.

Note: I have been recently told that a house has been built on or very near this old family burying ground.

THE HYMN-SINGING GHOST OF KING MANSION

The old E.W. King mansion still stands tall and proud, located on the southwest corner of Seventh and Anderson Streets near downtown Bristol, Virginia/Tennessee. Though this house faces Anderson Street, it has always been known as 308 Seventh Street. Erected about 1903, it served as home to the King family for well over thirty years. In the mid-1930s, Mr. and Mrs. King decided to downsize a bit. It was then that they built a cottage-type house at 700 Haynes Street, Bristol, Tennessee. There they spent the rest of their years. This former home also still stands.

Soon after the Kings left the mansion, it was leased to Bishop L. and Cora E. Osborne. Mrs. Osborne, for some unknown reason, was called "Toad." This couple opened a boardinghouse there known as Fort Shelby Place. This operated for a few years, and then the Osbornes moved to 348 Moore Street in Bristol, Virginia.

Soon afterward, the King mansion was divided into apartments. At first, the floor plan was left original, with only four apartments. Years

Though Mrs. E.W. King has been dead for more than seventy years, there are times when her voice can be heard singing old hymns in the mansion in which she lived so long.

later, it was divided into several more apartments and so remained until the 1990s. In the late 1990s, it was purchased and ultimately donated to the Bristol Historical Association. It has remained vacant ever since.

It was soon after the death of Mrs. E.W. King (formerly Alice Millard) that ghostly happenings began to occur there. When the decision was made by the owners to divide the place into four apartments, only the two west-side apartments (both upstairs and down) were rented. A young couple moved into the upstairs apartment, while a local schoolteacher rented the one below. It was not long after this young couple moved upstairs that they were awakened one morning at 5:00 a.m. by the sound of a woman softly singing a well-known hymn in the hallway. Along with the singing, there were distinct knocks on the other bedroom doors. This continued room by room as the voice moved slowly down the hall toward the young couple's bedroom. Then came the knock on their door. The young husband jumped from the bed and cautiously opened the door just a crack. No one was there. He did hear footsteps going down the back stairway, with the song continuing on. The couple checked with the tenant downstairs later that morning, but she had heard nothing and thought that their imagination was getting the best of them.

This young couple, apprehensive about the situation, heard nothing more for about a month. Then the same thing happened again! This time the husband opened the bedroom door before the knocking, hymn-singing ghost reached it. The knock was heard, but he could clearly see by the hall light that no one was there. He slammed the door and told his wife that they were moving that day. They did.

This left the local schoolteacher alone in the very large old house. It wasn't long before her "imagination" got the best of her, too. She arose one morning just before daylight, and given that the house was now her domain, she opened wide the pocket doors to what had been the main parlor of the home (then being used as the living room of her apartment). From the front hall (more correctly, a reception area) came the low sound of a woman's voice singing the same hymn that the young couple had told her about. It was the well-known and beloved hymn "My Faith Looks Up to Thee." Greatly startled, she quickly switched on the light. There on the landing of the grand staircase stood a slightly stooped lady! It was clear that she was a dignified woman and appeared to be rather old. She was well dressed, her hair was done up in a bun and a lady's watch was suspended around her neck. Anyone who was well acquainted with Mrs. E.W. King would have known that this ghost was her, returning from the other world to again reign over her grand mansion. She had her arms stretched upward as she sang the old hymn in a low but strong voice. Dismissing the event as being only her imagination, the teacher closed the doors quickly and did not venture out of her room again until the welcome appearance of daylight.

Although a bit apprehensive, she continued living there for some time. The remaining apartments were soon filled, and all was well, with no sign of the ghost. One night, the ghost, not having appeared for several months, was seen and heard by the teacher again. This "repeat performance" was too much for her nerves, and she decided to move elsewhere. When the next tenant moved into the teacher's former apartment, the performance was repeated.

Perhaps a granddaughter of the Kings explained things when she, in the course of an ordinary conversation with one of the tenants, told of her grandmother's morning ritual. She described her late grandmother as always arising sharply at 5:00 a.m. to supervise the serving of breakfast. Just before breakfast was to be served, Mrs. King would travel up the front stairs to make the rounds to awaken the family. All the while she would softly sing her favorite old hymn, "My Faith Looks Up to Thee." The granddaughter added that Grandmother King, being a devout Christian woman, would often stand on the landing with arms outstretched and sing the first verse of this hymn. She supposed that the singing of the hymn in the morning would help fill the house with the presence of the Lord.

The house finally became vacant after being rented for many years. Soon afterward, it was sold to a man who came here from Maryland. He bought several fine old homes. About the time of the sale, strange lights began appearing in the dark house. Some thought that vagrants might have moved in and attributed the lights to them. However, the lights were always either blue or red and did not remain in one room. Instead, the lights would appear for a few seconds on one floor and then be seen instantly on another. The colors would often change as the lights zipped from floor to floor. Several reports were made of these sightings.

One night, a man parked his car at the back of the house to make a visit to a house across the street, returning about midnight. As he opened the car door, he was startled to hear the distinct sound of an organ playing somewhere in the darkened house. It was faint at first but grew louder and seemed to be moving closer to him. In seconds, he was in his car and quickly sped away. What was the organ playing? The man, a Presbyterian, recognized the song instantly as a familiar hymn played frequently in his church, "My Faith Looks Up to Thee."

About ten years ago, the house was given to the Bristol Historical Society by the gentleman from Maryland. It still remains vacant. There have been no reports of ghosts in recent years, but perhaps the singing of that old hymn will again be heard in the halls of that beautiful mansion.

THE SMOKING CHIMNEY GHOST

Ghostly appearances may take many forms, but not often does such appear as smoke. However, this did happen near Bristol several years ago and may even have been seen in very recent times.

Out where Old Jonesboro Road crosses Bristol Caverns Highway there yet stands an ancient log house. It appears to have been built in two sections. Likely, the smaller section was built first with an outside chimney. Later, a larger addition was added to the chimney end of the smaller and older cabin. This enclosed the chimney, thus creating what is often called a "saddleback house." As did many an old log house, it later sprouted a plank addition or two, and a full porch was added to the Jonesboro Road side. From a rather humble beginning, it finally evolved into a fairly commodious country home, and for many years it well served a highly respected Sullivan County, Tennessee family.

It is not likely, though, that a fire has been kindled on the old hearths of that house in three quarters of a century or longer. Several years ago, a lady living in that area was driving to her work in Bristol. Her day began very early, so daylight was just beginning to break when she neared the old and long-deserted house. In the dim light of that early dawning, she was startled to see heavy smoke billowing upward from the chimney and what appeared to be an oil lamp feebly flickering in one of the small windows.

Later that day, when she returned home, she told her mother that it appeared that someone had moved into the long-abandoned old house

Though no fires have been candled in the fireplaces of this old log home for many years, there are still times when smoke rises from the chimney.

at the crossroads. Her mother was one who always tried to keep abreast of the latest community happenings and soon called the owner of the property. She was told that no one had rented the house, and as far as he knew, there had been no fires kindled in the fireplace for many years. That caused the owner to become very concerned about the matter, and he hastened over to investigate. He found that those old fireplaces that had been cleaned out years ago had no sign of recent fires in them. This puzzled the owner, causing him to keep a closer watch on the unused house. Weeks, months and years passed without him seeing a thing unusual about the place. However, others did.

A rather large family rented a house just a short distance from this location. There came a heavy snowfall one night soon after they moved there. The next morning was bright but cold. Naturally, the children wanted to play in the newly fallen snow. In their play, they wandered down the road to the old house. By then, their hands and feet were becoming very cold. Seeing heavy smoke rolling up from the chimney of the old house, they decided to stop and see if whoever lived there would allow them inside to warm themselves by the fire. They found the door open but no one was in sight. No furnishings were in the room in which they looked. They went to the door leading to the other fireplace room but found it the same—no fire was burning yet smoke was rolling upward from the chimney.

Over the next few years, several others people reported seeing the unexplainable smoke rising up from the long-unused chimney. Then came a visitor to this area who may have shed light on the cause of the ghostly smoke.

The visitor was an old lady, likely then in her early nineties. She had come here for what she called her "last visit from her childhood." She was reared within a short distance of the old log house at the crossroads. While here, she talked much about happenings that took place when she was a young lady living nearby (this was more than eighty years before). Among other things, she told of a tragedy that had occurred in the house. The family living there then took in a homeless man to live with them. In time, he became demented, and plans were made to send him to an insane asylum. During those trying days, he was seldom left alone.

A day came, however, when this demented man's only guardian was a late teenage son of the family. Others of the family had gone to nearby Bristol. A friend of this son soon came along the Old Jonesboro Road riding a fine, recently purchased horse. He called for the boy to come out and see his much-prized acquisition. Reluctantly, he did go out to the yard fence but not before he firmly told his charge to remain in his chair and not go near the fireplace (the man had the habit of stirring the fire and adding wood when such was not needed). The horse was indeed a beauty, causing the lad to stay outside longer than he intended. When he turned back toward the house, he was startled to see a strange-colored smoke rolling upward from the chimney. Thinking that the old man was stirring the fire, he raced in to investigate the matter. Once inside, he found a ghastly scene. His charge was not stirring the fire. He had become part of it! The tottering old fellow had fallen face first into the large fireplace, and it was too late to save him.

"Land!" the old lady exclaimed and continued:

> *I was taken over there by my folks real soon after that awful thing happened and I can smell that awful odor of burning flesh yet. They said it was a long time before it got out of that house and I recollect that smoke had settled all over the yard and it smelled awful too. They said*

the place was hainted after that. We left here soon after that happened and moved to west Tennessee but someone wrote us that those folks would sometimes see smoke roll out of the chimney even in summertime and there'd be no fire in the fireplace and that awful odor would begin again.

On Christmas Day 2003, a well-known resident of Bristol, Tennessee, was driving home on Bristol Caverns Highway. At the crossroads, he turned right on the Old Jonesboro Road. He well knew the old landmark on his left had not been occupied for years, yet he was startled to see a strange-colored smoke rolling upward from the rapidly deteriorating chimney. A strange, nauseating odor suddenly filled the car, even though all the windows were tightly closed. Other folks have recently reported similar experiences.

This author has written of more than one "smelling ghost"; however, this is his first story of one made of smoke.

TERROR IN THE BATHROOM

Of all the rooms in the house, the one that should be most "ghost free" is the bathroom. The reader may draw his or her own conclusions as to why. Unfortunately, there are at least three bathrooms in this city, all in Tennessee, that are what I call "severely haunted." For fear of stirring the ire of the property owners, I cannot reveal the exact locations of any of them. Even without exact addresses, be assured that those individuals written of here and experiencing those ghostly events swear that they are very, very real.

One happened not so far from Tennessee High School. A family was renting a modest cottage. They found their new home satisfying, at least for a few days. On a snowy January morning, the wife was left alone there. The husband had gone to work, and given that the snow was not so heavy or deep, the children had gone off to school. The woman, now with a quiet house, took the paper and went to the bathroom for what she thought would be a restful respite from the duties of the day. She closed the door but did not lock it. In a few minutes, that door was suddenly thrown open. That was shock enough, but what she then saw was far more so.

Before her stood a wild-eyed, bushy-haired man with an old-fashioned straight razor in his hand. The poor woman froze in terror, thinking that she was surely going to be attacked and killed. Instead, he attacked himself. He raised the razor and slashed his throat from ear to ear. The last she remembered was blood flowing down his white shirt as he crumpled to the floor. When she finally came to, everything appeared normal—no bloody body, no door flung open, nothing. Dressed in only her housecoat, she shot out the front door and wildly ran through the snowy streets to her sister's home two blocks away. She was never in that house again. The family moved out that afternoon.

The police were summoned, and it was then that they learned the rest of the story. When the police arrived, they found nothing; however, both veteran policemen on the scene remembered that what the woman had seen had actually happened in that bathroom some four or five years before. The woman had seen a ghostly reenactment of that tragic event. What makes this so thought-provoking to me and perhaps to the reader is that the woman had no knowledge of the suicide that had taken place in that bathroom, and therefore no one could say that it was an imagined event. The reader may draw his or her own conclusions in this matter.

PART VI

PROPHETS, WARNINGS AND WITCHES

THE WARNING LIGHT IN EAST HILL CEMETERY

My mother always said that she did not believe in ghosts; however, she did believe in warnings. She would often tell of strange happenings that had occurred to foretell the deaths of just about every member of her father's family.

It seems that there have been "warning ghosts" in Bristol. I have heard many stories along this line. The first I heard after coming to Bristol was told to me by one of my welfare clients. I will here share it with you.

Though the subject of this story had no burial lot in East Hill Cemetery, he did have ancestral ties there. His maternal line ran to the DePrato family, early settlers of Bristol who are buried in this historic cemetery. Perhaps that is why a warning or prophetic ghost appeared to him as he drove by there one foggy night in the early 1940s.

For two or three years, he had passed that cemetery every work night at about 10:45 p.m., driving from his home on East State Street to the local railroad yards to begin his night shift there.

On one particular night, he had just made it through the intersection at the east end of the cemetery when something like a large spotlight appeared from the cemetery at the right side of his car. It began moving along with him, blinking three times, pausing and blinking three times again. He sped up but so did the ghostly light. He floored the car in fear, but the ghostly light sped up to stay with him. The light wasn't confined

The warning light passed between the monument to the town's founder and the southern fence of the East Hill Cemetery.

to the end of the cemetery either but continued right on down the hill until it reached the intersection with Short Street. There, it seemed to explode, with bits of bright light flying in all directions. This experience so disturbed him that he could hardly attend to his duties in the railroad yard that night.

The next night, as he drove to work, the same experience occurred, but with a slight difference. Instead of blinking three times, the light only blinked twice. After reporting this, the man's wife begged and pleaded with him not to go the same route on the third night. She felt that he was seeing a warning ghost and that something would happen on that third trip to work.

We will never know if the light appeared that third night or not. All we know is that at the intersection of Short and State Streets, a car, driven by a drunken man, shot out of Short Street and hit the haunted man's car broadside, creating an awful wreck in which both men were killed. When his widow told me this story, she called it a "warning ghost," and I could not help remembering my mother telling me of warnings that had happened in her family long, long ago. The widow told me that she never again passed East Hill Cemetery after dark. Beware, readers, and take heed!

STRANGE POWERS

Along with these ghost stories, I think it's fitting to include a bit about some local persons who seem to have strange, unearthly powers. Yes, Bristol has always had its share of such people. Most were women of varying degrees of capability and local fame. Some were obscure, with nothing else to distinguish them. Others were well known and long remembered for other activities.

Among the latter was Pocahontas Hale, longtime operator of Bristol's largest brothel, the Black Shawl. Space does not permit the enumeration of all of her strange works, but I will here include a sampling that will give an idea of those powers that made her so unusual.

Pocahontas Hale emerged as a psychic when she began to locate well sites for local homebuilders. She used no divining rod. Instead, she simply walked about, looking intently at the ground and lowly muttering strange, unintelligible words. She then would suddenly stop. Her left leg would do an automatic up and down "jerk," stomping the ground. This was done in slow motion. If there were two stomps of her foot, water could be found at twenty feet. Three stomps meant thirty feet and so on. She traveled all over Bristol and the surrounding area, locating water at ten dollars per find. Old-timers claim that she was never wrong. She also picked up ten-dollar fees for locating and identifying unknown and unmarked Confederate graves buried here during the Civil War. I could show you one stone with an inscription that was put there because Pocahontas claimed that a soldier was buried in that location.

An interesting story involving two psychic visions caused a dam building project to be halted. The town fathers planned the dam on Beaver Creek between Fairview Avenue and Norfolk Street. It would have been slightly upstream from the Mary Street crossing of Beaver Creek. Pocahontas foresaw that it would someday break and ruin downtown Bristol. Another local woman had an identical vision concerning this calamity. Strangely, these two women despised the sight of each another, and no wonder—the other was the legendary Rosetta Bachelor, the town's super and militant moralist. It is strange that she agreed with the operator of the largest brothel here, but both claimed that during the same night, at the same time, a vision concerning this matter came to them. Their visions foretold that during the fourth new moon of the third year after the completion of this dam, there would be a prolonged cloudburst on the headwaters of Beaver that would cause this dam to break. The breaking of this dam would flood downtown Bristol. Both saw much damage to the buildings and large numbers of people drowned. By then, both women had proven their ability as "fortune tellers." The majority of the local citizens believed them, and the resultant pressure put on the town fathers caused the plan to be scrapped.

Rosetta Bachelor had established herself as a "seer" when, in 1858, she prophesied the beginning of the Civil War. According to Rosetta, it was to begin in April 1861. Of course, she was right. She also foretold the great Battle of Fredricksburg and gave the date and extensive details of the battle. She was again proven right.

Another local woman with "powers of prophesy" was "One Tooth" Pansy Bates. This widow long lived in a little cottage on old James Row. She survived by doing domestic work for the elite folks on Solar Hill, directly behind her home. Perhaps her best-remembered and long-talked-of prophesy was the foretelling of the death of Joseph R. Anderson, founder of this city. She predicted he would die in May 1888. When told of this, he shrugged it off and said that he had plans far beyond that time and expected to carry through on them. He didn't. He died on May 18, 1888. Old "One Tooth Pansy" attended the funeral, and some who were there declared that she had a pleased look on her face, as if to say, "See, I told you so."

I once found her name in a divorce file in the Abingdon, Virginia courthouse. It seems that she had a vision of a well-known Bristol businessman secretly visiting a "shady lady" in "Little Hell," a notorious slum at the end of Second Street. Her vision proved to be true. His wife filed for divorce and mentioned Pansy as her first source of information. Now Pansy also foretold her own demise and how it would happen. She

"One Tooth" Pansy Bates
foretold the death of Bristol's
founder, Joseph R. Anderson,
many months before it occurred.

said that she would die by drowning in Beaver Creek. In 1894, she tried
to wade Beaver Creek when it was swollen a bit from heavy rains. She
slipped on a slick rock and fell face forward and drowned before she
could regain her footing.

From time to time, many old residents of Bristol have told of a frightful
woman who lived somewhere on McDowell Street in Bristol, Tennessee.
She lived alone and had no family or friends. Everyone feared her and
stayed out of her way as much as possible. Some called her a witch,
but most referred to her as the "voodoo woman." Like Pocahontas, she
always wore jet-black headgear that almost covered her face. One elderly
woman, yet living, remembered that at twilight every day, this strange
and greatly feared woman would walk up McDowell Street, cross East
State and stand at the locked gate of East Hill Cemetery until darkness
fell (during that time, the cemetery was fenced and had locked gates).
While standing, she would steadily and intently look into the cemetery,
muttering some kind of incantation in what sounded like a foreign

language. Some said that she was drawing her powers by speaking with the dead who were buried in that historic old cemetery.

There were some locals who paid this "voodoo woman" to work "spells" on their enemies. It seems that one of her specialties (and probably the most profitable) was her ability to rein in unfaithful husbands. When paid ten dollars, an angry wife could ask her to work a spell on the erring husband rendering him completely impotent. Then, after six months and upon sworn promises that he would never stray again (and for further consideration of a twenty-dollar fee), she would release him from her "curse." She made considerable money in this manner. I have heard numerous other stories concerning this much-feared voodoo woman, but space will not permit the telling of them here. She died alone, had a pauper's burial with no funeral service and was buried in what was then called the potter's field of East Hill Cemetery. Could she be the ghostly woman in black who from time to time can been seen wandering around in that section of that old cemetery? Usually, this ghostly woman in black appears in broad daylight.

POCAHONTAS HALE WALKS AGAIN

I have told the story of Pocahontas Hale, who long operated Bristol's largest brothel. This was the Black Shawl and stood at 645 State Street, now the location of the Cameo Theatre. She stood about six feet tall, rather unusual for a woman, was slim as a beanpole and always stood very erect, so much so that one old-timer said she stood as if "tied to a fence rail." When walking about, she always looked straight ahead, never glancing left or right and never acknowledging anyone she might meet. She never even spoke when spoken to and once was described as a "walking statue" always dressing in jet-black. Her skirts touched the street. Always, summer or winter, she wrapped herself in an enormous black shawl (thus came the name of her establishment). Her headgear was a nondescript scarf covering her head, ears and neck all the way to the collar. Ol' Dad Thomas often said, "That ol' gal looked like a real haint, even if she was still alive, at least I think she was alive. She wore elbow-length jet-black gloves summer and winter. Indeed, all that could be seen of her real self was a bit of face and that portion of her skin was deathly white."

At the best, she did not, in the least, resemble a prominent madam. She looked more like someone's century-old grandmother who had escaped from a cemetery. Her extreme height for a woman, the size of her hands, gloved though they were, and her feet made many believe she was a man dressed as a woman. Adding to this belief was the depth of her voice, though she seldom spoke. Some thought that she might be a fugitive from justice and was concealing herself/himself from the law. If such a person appeared on the street now, she would certainly be noticed and probably questioned. Could it be that Pocahontas Hale, though now gone for over a century, is now coming back from the dead to stroll again near the site of her notorious business?

In late January 2003, a rather excited man came into the Bristol Public Library (only a short distance from the Cameo) and exclaimed that he'd just seen the ghost of Pocahontas Hale. Evidently, he had read of her in one of my books. He later admitted that he would never plan to go walking by the Cameo again. This occurred in broad daylight.

A Bristol businesswoman, also walking near the Cameo, came upon what she called "this creature" that suddenly appeared from nowhere, walked a few steps and then disappeared right before her eyes.

This happened again two years later. This time, Pocahontas appeared to two teenagers walking along the street, and they, too, ran to the library, asking if perhaps I might be there. As it happened, I was there and was able to verify by the description they gave that they had indeed seen the old madam.

Sometime later, a local psychic woman went to

The Cameo Theatre occupies the lot on which Bristol's largest brothel operated. The madam of that brothel has been seen near there in recent times.

the spot near the Cameo about midnight for the purpose of calling up the spirit of Pocahontas Hale. She reported back that she was indeed successful and that the ghost did indeed answer her call, appear from the spirit world and stand close to her for perhaps half a minute and then just vanished away.

Beware! When you go walking near the Cameo, whether in daylight or darkness, you also may have an encounter with this historic ghost who does seem to appear there once in a while.

BRISTOL'S OLDEST PSYCHIC

Another claim that Bristol has of being a unique place is that it was once home to one who was reputed to be the "oldest man in the world." He was Silas ("Old Si") Goodson, a slave owned by the pioneer King family. He always said that his mother told him that he was born under a blooming apple tree because it was so hot in her windowless cabin. Thus, we can say that he was born in the spring of the year, or "apple blooming time," though the exact date is not known. Good evidence indicates that he was born about 1730 in either Lunningburg or Prince Edward County, Virginia, and purchased by Major Thomas Goodson, who later moved to Floyd County, Virginia. The purchase was made in 1760. In the old bill of sale, Silas was said to be "sound of body and mind and was about 28–30 years old and was a slave for life." Doubtless, Major Goodson never imagined that the life of that slave would extend for more than a century from the time of that purchase.

Another witness to the age of Old Si was Sarah, a daughter of Major Goodson's. She was born in 1765. Her clear memory of this slave began about 1770. She told that at that time he was about forty years old and remembered that he had children who were in their late teens and early twenties (there would be many more children before his long life ended). She recalled that he was a highly valued slave of her father's, who had trained him to be a carpenter and brick mason. When this Sarah married Colonel James King, Old Si was given to her as part of her dowry. Her father supposed that a trained builder would be valuable to the young couple as they sought to establish a home in the wilderness that is now Bristol, Tennessee. His supposition proved to be very correct, not only for

Old Si Goodson, once thought to be the oldest man in the world, is buried in the slave section of East Hill Cemetery. He is reputed to have had remarkable psychic powers.

the immediate future but for many years to come as well. Indeed, Old Si did help build the King's first home at Holly Bend, which is about four miles down Beaver Creek from the heart of present Bristol.

In 1816–17, he did the brickwork on the James King Jr. home in present Bristol, Virginia. A small portion of that home still stands at 54 King Street, though it has been much added to over the passing years (actually, only two rooms of the original home still stand). There is an exposed wall at the back where his handiwork can still be viewed. He made the brick for that house from a clay pit a short distance down the hill toward the present Bristol Public Library. He was in his mid-eighties when the King house was constructed; at ninety years of age he did the brickwork for the Presbyterian church at Paperville, Bristol, Tennessee. Long before the building of these notable structures, Colonel King had taught Old Si another trade—iron making. He soon became so talented at this trade that he was called an iron master. About 1821, Colonel King moved him to the ironworks at Shady Valley, Tennessee. There he became an assistant to William King, the unmarried son of the colonel. It was while living in that high mountain valley that he began to exhibit strange psychic powers, so much so that some of the neighbors began to fear him, saying that he was a witch.

The first recounted "prophesy" of Old Si's came about noon on August 17, 1825. He came running in from a cornfield, excitedly calling to master William that his father (Colonel King) had just died. "I seed it all in a vision," he exclaimed and went on to say "the Colonel is now lying dead under a huge tree near a big river." William, thinking that the old slave was becoming a bit demented, paid little attention to what he was saying. Just after dark that night, a messenger rode up before the house with the news that Colonel King had died about noon that day. He went on to tell that the colonel had died while lying under a huge shade tree beside the river of what is now Bluff City, Tennessee.

Later that fall, during corn harvesting time, William King casually mentioned that he would like to have some good venison to eat. "A big deer will come into this field at sunset," Old Si replied, "and I'll wait here to get him." The big deer did come, and William had fresh venison the next day.

While living in Shady Valley, Old Si seemed to develop a keen interest in living to be very old. While stretched out on the porch taking a nap one summer afternoon, he (as he later told it) had a vision that was as clear and bright as the summer sun. He said that he was told in that vision that if he wanted to live a long life, he would have to sleep in the open air all year long, eat at least a quart of honey every day and wash it down with buttermilk. He also "saw" in the vision to dip himself three times in water every day of the year, regardless of temperature.

When he reported this to master William, he was told he could have the honey if he could locate the hives in the trees in the woods. This was no problem to Old Si. He just looked slowly around the rim of Shady Valley and said, "They's three big trees in a row up yonder on Laurel Ridge, and they are loaded with golden honey." The master well knew that Old Si had never been on top of that ridge. Nevertheless, William accompanied Silas and went up to that ridge; sure enough, three large trees stood in a row and were loaded with honey. From that day on, this slave had his portion of milk and honey. He also started dipping three times in water every morning, often before daylight and in all kinds of weather. "That icy water makes me come alive," he would say. He never missed a night sleeping in open weather, either, even when chilling winds blew down from the high ridges above Shady Valley.

In the summer of 1844, William King became ill. Somehow, he sensed that he would not live much longer. He called his faithful old slave to his side and asked him to see, when death came, that his body be taken back to Holly Bend on Beaver for burial in the family cemetery. He added that he hoped it would be in warm weather so the trip would not be so unpleasant. "No master William," the slave replied, "it won't be in warm weather, but I will take you anyway, though it will be hard cold and snow will be deep on the ground." In mid-December that year, William King died. Snow lay deep on the ground, and the temperature was near zero. As darkness crept over the valley that night, Old Si and six other young, strong slaves began the long journey back to Holly Bend. The coffin was swung under a pole born on the shoulders of the strong slaves, including Old Si. All through that frigid night, the men pressed on, down the snow-covered mountain and across the Holston Valley. At daylight, they arrived at the old family cemetery on Beaver. Silas had kept his promise to master William. The nearly 112-year-old slave was cold and tired, but apparently no more so than his younger companions. Old Si never returned to Shady Valley but rather was taken into the home of Reverend James King, living then at what is now Solar Hill in Bristol, Virginia.

At his new location, Old Si continued his milk and honey diet, slept in the open and dipped himself in nearby Beaver Creek early every morning. His dipping place was at the mouth of a short spring branch that entered Beaver directly in front of the new library in downtown Bristol. This place was called "The Prophet's Hole" long after this slave had died.

It was very uncommon to allow a slave to carry a gun, but Old Si was a highly trusted slave and always a successful hunter. If the family craved a wild turkey, he would say, "Well there's one over yonder in the knobs a-sittin' on a low limb just waitin' for me." A little later, he would come home with a fat turkey. He "divined" bee trees so much that in time there were nearly two hundred hives in the bee yard behind the old King house on Solar Hill.

One cold morning in 1846, Silas arose and told the family that ten years from that time there would be the coldest winter ever experienced in the area. The winter of 1856 was indeed very long and severely cold. I have here at Pleasant Hill a letter noting that the ground wasn't seen for nearly three months and that temperatures fell to well below zero every night. The new town had suffered for bread because the mill wheels were locked in ice, thus no grinding could be done.

Now James King had a son, William King, named for his uncle, who was studying to be a doctor. However, when the Mexican War broke out, he left his studies and went off to serve as a volunteer (while in the army, he did continue studying under an older surgeon). Finally, the war ended. A letter arrived at the James King home stating that William would soon be home. This caused the family to greatly rejoice. But Old Si was not rejoicing. Indeed, he seemed rather sad. Finally, he spoke up and said, "No, Mr. William will not be coming home. We'll never see him again. I done had a dream last night, clear as the morning. I seed him going down, down, down in deep water, and mountains of water were closing over him." William King was returning by ship to New Orleans when, about three days from the port, he became very ill and died. He was buried at sea. Indeed, he went down, down, down, and mountains of water did close over him.

All through the years, this aged slave continued to work alongside the younger men and women on the King plantation. Nothing was too hard for him. Once he had his honey and buttermilk and his dip in Beaver, he would enter into whatever duty was at hand with "gusto." His eyesight remained very sharp, and he never lost a tooth in his long life. His hair never turned gray but remained as black as when young. He could climb the steepest hills in a lively manner and never become short of breath.

Topping all his prophetic statements was one concerning the future of the heart of King's plantation, most of what was generally known as Kings Meadows. One morning, in mid-spring 1845, he arose a bit earlier than usual. James King, always a very early riser, was already up and strolling about his four-acre yard. The excited old slave came running to him and told him of his latest "night vision." This vision foretold that before many years had passed, a bustling city would spread over the meadows and cultivated fields that lay along the meandering Beaver Creek in front of King's big house. "Someday you can stand right here and see it! Last night, I saw thousands of candles flickering in the valley, and I heard the sound of a thousand trumpets splitting the darkness followed by a roaring storm moving along the far edge of the big meadow. A city will fill that valley just as sure as you live." In later years, the Kings reasoned the "thousands of candles" Old Si had seen foreshadowed city lights and that the "trumpets followed by the roaring storm" meant the passing of trains through the city that was to come. Old Si even went so far to say that he had been shown that he would take part in the beginning of this city.

After James King began building his new home near present Melrose Street on Beaver, Old Si told him he wouldn't always live there. "Master King, you'll spend your last days living on the old feed lot," he would say with a sound of certainty. The feedlot was a place on the edge of the big meadow where the cattle were fed. This made little sense to Reverend King.

In August 1852, surveyors entered the King plantation and began to lay out the town of Bristol that would become the city of the prophet's dream. Old Si Goodson served as a chain bearer. Indeed, he did take part in the beginning of this city, just as he had prophesied. Before long, there would be lights in the valley, and trains would sound out with a blast of trumpets and the sound of a roaring storm would follow behind them.

The old feedlot Si had predicted would be the site of a home became the northeast corner of State and Moore. Ten years later, 1862, James King bought the house that was located on the old feedlot, and this indeed was his last home. While yet living on Beaver, James King expressed the hope that he was in his last dwelling place. "The last setting sun that I see will be over the knobs beyond my home," he once said. Old Si heard him say it and, having had another of his frequent visions, said to his master, "No, the last setting sun you will see will not be over the knobs. When the sun goes down on your last day it will be over a row of tupelo trees at the end of the mile-long cotton rows in a far distant place." This impressed James King, for he knew that Old Si had never seen a tupelo tree nor likely had ever heard of one. In July 1867, Reverend King went on a trip to Monroe County, Mississippi, to visit his daughter and son-in-law, who lived on a large strawberry plantation. While there, he suddenly died. The last sunset he saw was indeed over a row of tupelo trees at the end of mile-long cotton rows. The last prophecy made by his old, faithful and highly valued slave was fulfilled.

And what of Old Si Goodson's final fate? In the spring of 1862, he took his gun, slung his powder horn over his shoulder and went down Beaver to hunt awhile. He also took a hoe to dig some spice wood roots for his medicine-making (among other things, he was a noted herb doctor). He returned about noon and found the house in great agitation. In his absence, a band of bushwhackers (the Civil War was then raging) had attacked the place and taken away much of the provisions. They also took two of the slave girls. One of these was a granddaughter of his. They had gone up the knobs behind the King home. Greatly angered, he immediately took off after them. He reached the first bank of the knobs. There his 132-year-old heart gave out. He fell forward on his gun and powder horn and breathed his last. Down in the valley, numerous apple trees were in full bloom. He had been born in apple blossom time and had died in the same season about 130 to 132 years later. Folks had long been calling him the "oldest man in the world." Was he? The question still lingers.

As an added note, I will here say that the place where he fell dead would now be in the yard of Belvedere Mansion on the hill above Ninth Street. He was first buried in a little slave cemetery that was located on the corner of Rose and Seventh Streets. Several years later, it was thought necessary to remove the bodies buried there. Joseph Anderson, a son-in-law of James King's, had Old Si moved to the lot at the northern edge of East Hill Cemetery that had been set aside for slave burials. There, in the recently restored slave plot, rests one who supposedly was the "oldest man in the world."

THE VOODOO WOMAN APPEARS AGAIN

In another story in this book, I told of the "voodoo woman" who once terrorized people by her supposed power to work spells. She was greatly feared by the local citizens. She had the unnerving habit of slipping up behind unsuspecting folks and screeching out "Voodoo! Voodoo!" This, as could well be expected, put these folks into sudden flight.

Ol' Dad Thomas once told me how his wife went visiting on McDowell Street one day. It was getting dark when she started home. She had gone only a short distance when she heard the woman screaming out behind her, "Voodoo! Voodoo!" Mrs. Thomas ran hard for more than a mile and fell in on the home porch gasping out, "The voodoo woman is after me!" Evidently, the feared woman had given up the chase long before she reached the Thomas home.

Many other stories have been told to me of similar nature, but perhaps this will suffice to indicate to the reader the constant terror this crazed woman had over the townsfolk of Bristol.

No one seems to know when the voodoo woman died. I have had speculative guesses all the way from about 1915 to sometime during the Great Depression. One old lady swore it was during the great flu epidemic of 1918. Whenever the date, it is known that she did die alone and very poor. She had no known relatives. Most folks were afraid to be near her even when she was dead, but a few brave men put together a plain, no-frills box made of lumber left over from an old side room that had been torn from a nearby house. She had been dead three days or more when found. Fortunately, the weather was cold. One man who helped with the making of the coffin and burial who was yet living when I came here told me about it, and I will write it just as he said it:

When we got that thar box ready, we just flopped her down in it. She still had on those old black clothes she died in like she always wore. We then just nailed the lid down on it and carried her over to the East Hill Cemetery and buried her afore dark. There wasn't no preaching nor praying nor anything like that. All thought she was the devil's daughter anyway so we just buried her, and hurried to get it done because we wanted to git out of that cemetery afore dark come. We didn't even take time to stick a rock at the old grave spot.

The voodoo woman was buried very near Williams Street in an area that is now grown over with brush and saplings. This area in which she is buried has become a favorite spot for youth to play around in, and some still do. Years ago, on a balmy spring day, three or four boys went into those woods with toy guns playing like they were hunting. They hunted up more than they expected. As they strolled along, they suddenly heard a voice behind them screaming "Voodoo! Voodoo!" They whirled around. Coming toward them was a black, draped figure. All that was

This is the only known picture of Bristol's notorious voodoo woman.

85

visible was a face, but the face had no flesh! It was a skeleton! The voice continued to cry out "Voodoo! Voodoo!" as the ghost ran toward them. Those boys took off like a streak of lightning.

Years later, one of those boys, by then a grown man and working with a local construction crew, told me that back then he was beyond the railroad yard and still running when he, as he expressed it, "got his mind back." You may be sure that none of those boys ever forgot that ghostly experience.

Some time later, a man was driving along the woods down Williams Street. As he passed by, a skeleton dressed in black jumped out into the road. It appeared that the man would surely run over whatever it was. Instead, the figure leapt on the hood of his car and screeched out "Voodoo! Voodoo!" In absolute terror, the man lost control of the car and whipped back and forth across the road, ending up in the ditch. The car stopped, but the man sure didn't! He jumped out and hit the ground running. For as long as he lived, he would never drive by those woods again, not even in broad daylight.

I think it was in my third year here (1956) that there was another dramatic appearance of the voodoo woman. About that time, there was a rash of vandalism in East Hill Cemetery. Consequently, the management asked the local police department to patrol the cemetery at night. Given that the cemetery is located in both cities, each side of the city cooperated in the matter. About 1:00 a.m., a Virginia policeman was slowly driving along what is now Hugh Hagan Drive. As he was about level with the area the voodoo woman is buried, he heard a voice call out "Voodoo! Voodoo!" It sounded as if the voice came from just down the hill below the driveway where he was moving along. He instantly turned his spotlight in that direction, and there, just a few feet away, stood a figure clad in black. As he looked, it started coming toward him. As it approached, he saw the figure wasn't human. Indeed, it was a skeleton!

Years later, this policeman frankly told me that he realized there was no use trying to arrest something "out of this world" and further confessed that he was so frightened that he "shot the gas to it" and headed for the cemetery gate. The very next day, he got himself changed to the day shift and was not in that cemetery after dark again.

In recent years, there have been a few reports of a black-clad figure appearing near the area where the voodoo woman is buried, and these have been daylight sightings. There is no telling what might be seen there at night.

THE WHITE FLAG FLYING

Near Christmas 1953, the late James King Brewer, then near ninety years old, sat in his commodious old home at 220 Johnson Street and told me this story. He was a solid, well-educated and highly respected senior citizen of Bristol. Certainly, he was not one given to idle tales. He is what I would call a "credible witness."

On June 11, 1918, a neighbor of Mr. Brewer's (living just across from the Brewer home) on the east side of Johnson Street in Bristol, Virginia, ate his breakfast and took a seat in his front upstairs bedroom to watch the goings-on in the neighborhood. This was the man's usual daily practice (long before the days of television). He was not beyond walking about his neighborhood but seldom did so. His little world consisted mainly of what he saw from that large upstairs window. That day, he saw far more than he expected.

The day had dawned bright and fair. Not a breeze was blowing, and there was promise in the air of a pleasant, mild day ahead. Naturally,

The strange white flag was seen atop this old house that yet stands in Bristol, Virginia. It coincided with the death of a soldier who was raised in the home.

sitting in his window, he had a full view of the Brewer home. Mr. Brewer, prosperous and respected citizen of Bristol, had built this grand home about 1900. There he was rearing a fine family. Sadness, however, hung like a pall over that home, as it did over so many Bristol homes at the time. The nation was at war, and a fine, promising son of the Brewer family was serving in the U.S. Army. Last word from him was that he was in France and playing a very important role in the push toward the German border.

All of this may have been on the gentleman's mind that morning as he sat looking at his neighbor's house across the street. Bathed in the early morning sunlight, it took on a greater degree of grandeur than it did in later hours. At the very highest peak of the roof of this house was a tall, bright lightning rod. Many houses were equipped with such devices in those days. The man was looking up at the spherical rod when there suddenly appeared something sailing directly toward him. At first he thought it to be a large, white bird. Looking closer, he saw that it was a shining white flag, around which was a black border. Although the morning was perfectly still, the flag seemed to be propelled along by a brisk breeze. In moments, it attached itself to the lightning rod and there unfurled like a regular flag on its staff. It then detached itself, floated around the roof of the Brewer house and then sailed away to the west. Shortly, it appeared again, but this time it circled the house above the roof line, rising high with each circle, sailing high to the lightning rod and there again began to wave briskly in a still breeze.

By then, the old man decided that he was seeing something unearthly. He called downstairs to a grandson, telling him to go over and inform the Brewers that something strange was going on around their home. The grandson went and the entire family came outdoors and looked, but nothing could be seen. The black-bordered flag had vanished, never to appear again.

Mr. Brewer told me that he had no doubt that the gentleman in the house across the street was telling the truth, for within a few days word came that the soldier-son who was away in the war was killed on that very day, indeed at the very hour the strange white and black-bordered flag appeared over this family home.

As a matter of information, the Brewer's son was James Carlock Brewer, born on May 6, 1896, and was killed on January 11, 1918. The James C. Brewer Post of the American Legion in Bristol is named for him.

PART VII

HUMOROUS HAINTS AND THE LIVELY DEAD

GHOST HOG IN THE SMOKEHOUSE, OR NO BACON FOR BREAKFAST

This story was told to me in 1987 by the late Martha Jane Hart, who had lived most of her life on King College Road, at first near but later in Bristol, Tennessee. The setting of this story is near what we now call Goosepimple Junction.

When old Charley Barnes came into his kitchen for breakfast on that chilly morning way back there some time in 1910, he found that the daily bacon was not on the table. In those days, many Bristol-area farmsteads still had smokehouses in their backyards. Some housewives went to those smokehouses the night before to bring in meat for the next day. But Mrs. Barnes was different. She always went before daylight every morning for that purpose. On that particular morning, she had taken a little oil lamp, had gone into the smokehouse and was slicing off a generous portion of breakfast bacon when she heard a noise in the back of that little building. Just then, there came running toward her a large glowing white hog. He was grunting loudly and snapping his teeth. She well knew that there was no live hog in that building, certainly not one that was glowing like a white light. In terror, she sprang toward the back porch, leapt through the screen door and slammed and locked it behind her.

This woman met a ghost hog in her smokehouse. It is told that she never ate a bite of pork after this strange incident.

When her hungry husband came into the kitchen, not only was there no bacon on the table, there was nothing else either. Instead of finding the expected food, he found his wife shaking in fear. She had sat down in a chair near the stove and was trembling as one who was freezing to death. When she told him about what she called the "white ghost hog," he scoffed and boldly proclaimed that he was not afraid to go out there and "bring in the bacon." He went, but he did not "bring in the bacon." He found the smokehouse in flames. Evidently, in her frenzied fear, she had flung the lamp at the charging ghost hog, and this had set the building on fire. There was plenty of fried bacon that morning, but it was not on the table.

THE GHOST RATTLESNAKE

In my many years of listening to and reading ghost tales, I have learned of ghostly appearances in the form of dogs, cats, chickens (mostly crowing roosters), horses and even a cow or two. But only once have I heard of a rattlesnake ghost, and that happened right here in Bristol, Tennessee.

Several years ago, a lady living near the mouth of Steele's Creek was preparing to have her church circle meeting at her home. Her husband was taking their children out for a late lunch so as to clear the home for the planned meeting. Three of the women had come early in preparation for serving refreshments. The husband was a little late in getting home and was still taking his bath when the other ladies began to arrive. One of the ladies was entertaining the children in the kitchen while they waited for their daddy to take them out.

Meanwhile, in the bathroom, the husband was relaxing in a tub of hot, soapy water—that is, until suddenly he heard the distinct sound of a rattlesnake just to the right of the tub. Being a native of Lowndes County, Georgia, where such serpents abound, he knew the sound well. He also knew the look of the dangerous diamondback variety. That is just what he thought he saw coiled at the side of his bathtub! When he jerked his head in that direction to be certain, the head of that giant rattler was right in his face with his forked tongue flickering against his nose. There was a low whistling sound that is not natural to rattlesnakes, but he didn't take time to think of that. The snake was so large that it was unreal. He always vowed that the coil of that snake was as big as a washtub. It seems that the "preservation instinct" completed possessed him. In a split second, with super strength, he sprang from the tub over the coiled snake, landed near the door and sprinted right into the living room, where most of the women were assembled. All the while, he was yelling out, "There's a rattlesnake in the bathroom! It's a diamond-backer!"

The diamondback rattler is not a native species of Tennessee, but no one remembered that fact. Those women in the living room, perhaps more shocked by the nude man than the scream of a purported rattlesnake being nearby, became greatly excited. Some fainted, some jumped up and fled into the yard and some just sat looking straight ahead in wide-eyed surprise. The wife, who came running from the kitchen, was devastated by her husband's unusual behavior before the club and ran right to the bathroom. No snake was there. A couple of male neighbors also came quickly and looked everywhere in the house but found nothing. Needless to say, there was no circle meeting that day.

The family, partly because of fear and partly ashamed by the husband's behavior, moved away a short time later. The house burned down soon after. Just why a ghost of a rattlesnake appeared in that particular house no one has been able to figure out. Could it be that out there in that great ghost world, wherever that may be, a dispatcher had a little mischievous notion? I suppose we will never know.

SLEEPING WITH A GHOST, OR MORE THAN SHE BARGAINED FOR

A few years ago, a prominent Bristol lady was tickled pink when she found just the right antique bed for which she had long been searching. The big, old, high poster bed was indeed a dream come true, and to top it off, she got it at what she called a "real bargain price." She had it delivered to her home as soon as possible and spent much time cleaning and polishing it to perfection. She also bought a very expensive new mattress set, dressed it with her finest linen and topped it off with the best spread in the house. But it was not just to be an ornamental piece. She vowed she would sleep on it the rest of her life.

As the proud new owner of such a gorgeous old bed, she retired a little early that first night after it had been made ready for occupancy. And she did not immediately turn out the bedside lamp but rather lay for a long time admiring the soaring and highly carved posts of that ancient, antique bed. Finally, she turned out the light and then slowly drifted off to sleep. Perhaps she was soon dreaming of her good fortune in acquiring such a fine example of a gilded past age. About midnight, she slowly awoke to the sound of heavy breathing and low groans, apparently coming from right beside her and accompanied by someone thrashing about. Greatly alarmed, she sprang from the bed and turned on the bedside lamp. Instantly, the sound ceased. No one was there. Long pondering the matter, she finally came to the conclusion that perhaps this was all a bad dream—a very real one to be sure. But she had experienced such realistic dreams before, so she turned out the light and lay down, hoping that the "bad dreams" were over for the night.

About an hour later, she was awakened again by the same sounds. Again, turning on the lights caused the strange sounds to stop. That time, she stayed up a good while, but again she decided that maybe she was having a recurring nightmare similar to what she heard others speak of and perhaps had experienced before. Then she determined that when she laid down this time and turned the light off she would stay awake awhile just to be sure. Staying awake would not be hard to do. She was becoming rather tense and edgy about the matter. Acute anxiety had just about erased any drowsiness she might have had. For about an hour she lay staring into the darkness of her "silent as a tomb" bedroom. Then,

Pictured here is the Bristol, Virginia house where a woman discovered that she was sleeping with a ghost. It was demolished several years ago.

convinced that this had all been a vivid nightmare, she turned herself toward the lamp side of the bed, snuggled into the pillow and began a slow descent into that wonderful world of sleep. Hopefully, it would be dreamless sleep.

Then it happened! First came the feel of heavy breathing, with an icy-cold breath on the back of her neck. Almost instantly came the accompanying sounds along with agonizing groans and even more thrashing about, so much so that the bed covers were jerked from her. The realization hit her. She was really in bed with a ghost! As that realization shot through her mind, she shot out of bed. That time she did not bother with the bedside lamp. She leapt across the darkened room and ran into the door facing—knocking herself down—but she instantly was up and going again. In her nightclothes she fled to a neighbor's house and would not return home until broad daylight.

Before noon that day, she was back to the shop where the haunted bed had been bought. After a long siege of grueling interrogation, the dealer finally admitted that the bed did indeed have a gruesome past. He had bought it at an estate sale in southern Alabama. The former owner had been stabbed to death while in a drunken stupor on that bed. Indeed, there were dark stains on the lower part of the headboard that were thought to be splatters of blood from that poor victim. Now the dealer would not take it back, for he said that some strange sounds had come from it while it was in the shop, but he offered to help her find a buyer. That wasn't so hard to do, for the price was quickly slashed to less than half the original cost. Before the day was over, another Bristolian had hauled it away, so very happy with what he considered a "steal." In fact, he boasted to a friend that he "had skinned that poor woman alive." Well, it was soon learned that the bed had been sold again at an even greater reduced price! As to the final outcome of where the bed finally went, whether it was sold to another person or thrown in the city dump, I do not know.

Though this woman continued to buy antiques, she would never buy another antique bed. In fact, when she died, she was using a new, ultramodern bed. The author knows that to be fact, for he at one time owned the bed, and it was not haunted.

A parting word: please do let this story depress the sale of antique beds in Bristol or elsewhere. This author has owned numerous ancient beds. Indeed, he now sleeps on one that has been in service for more than 140 years! Not once has he had a ghostly experience while doing so.

CHASED BY A DEAD MAN

Bristol would not soon forget the time when a local woman thought that she was being chased by a dead man. Though this exciting event occurred about 1879, the story was still being told when I arrived here in 1953. It was told to me by Ol' Dad Thomas, who was then almost ninety-eight years old. He was an eyewitness of the excitement that this supposition caused.

In books past, I have written much about A.H. Bickley, Bristol's very flamboyant, never-to-be-forgotten undertaker. His wife, Harriet Ellen Bickley, has seldom ever been mentioned. She was a quiet, very retiring, humble woman who did not really enjoy being with people. However, she did assist her husband in some of his funeral services, but she confided to a friend that these public appearances were sheer torture to her. But there was a time when she made quite a public appearance right downtown in broad daylight, and that in a very pronounced manner.

One of Harriet's duties was to clean and decorate her husband's funeral parlor. For the purpose of decoration, she always kept a fine yard full of beautiful flowers. She also had many artificial flowers for use when real flowers were out of season. I have heard old-timers comment on the beauty of the Bickley homeplace. This was located just beyond the site of the First Christian Church on what is now Martin Luther King Boulevard. It was then known as Railroad Street. Just north of the home was Bickley's funeral parlor.

Mrs. H.A. Bickley said that her nerves were never steady after she was chased by a supposed dead man.

Mr. Bickley had a friend who lived on East Main (State) Street: Dan Beasley. Mr. Beasley was prone to having trouble with his neighbor. These disputes finally reached the place where the neighbor had vowed to kill Beasley. One day, after a severe dispute the night before, the two met down on Front Street, and there the trouble erupted again. The neighbor pulled a gun on Beasley and told him he was going to "lay him in the dust." At that point, Beasley began a flight toward Bickley's Hill (north along old Front Street called Virginia Hill, but for the sake of clarity, we will here call it Bickley's Hill). The man actually fired a shot at the fleeing neighbor, but the shot went wild. Near the crossing of Beaver Creek, the man stumbled and fell. It was fortunate that he did, for this gave Dan Beasley time to gain ground. He raced up the hill and rounded the curve to Bickley's funeral parlor. He rushed into the door and quickly told Mr. Bickley that he was being pursued by a would-be murderer and wanted to hide in the cellar. Mr. Bickley had a different idea. He considered the safest place to hide his friend was inside a display casket on view in the parlor. Beasley reluctantly agreed and climbed in, with Bickley shutting the lid down over him. Bickley then quickly placed an artificial wreath of flowers on the lid. Hardly had this been done when the gunman burst through the front door and began searching the place for Beasley. Of course, he did not go near the casket, thinking it contained the body of someone ready for burial. He soon gave up the search and hastened up the street hoping to find Beasley somewhere along the way.

Just as soon as he left, Harriet Bickley, having no knowledge of prior events, came in to begin her cleaning duties. Mr. Bickley, who had been standing outside watching the "enemy," turned back into the room as his wife began cleaning. Mrs. Bickley later said that she thought it strange that a casket being readied for burial would be in the parlor, for she did not remember hearing of anyone being brought in the day before. At the time, she thought nothing more about it. She approached the casket to better arrange the flowers, knowing that her husband was not the one usually assigned that duty. Meanwhile, inside the casket, poor Mr. Beasley was feeling the need for fresh air. Given that everything had quieted down, he correctly assumed that all was clear. He was also becoming panicked, thinking that he would be smothered.

Just as Harriet Bickley was arranging the flowers, the lid was thrown back, causing the flowers to fly against the wall. Beasley popped up right in her face, saying, "I've got to have air. I'd just as soon be shot as to smother to death!" Mr. Bickley later described what happened from there. His wife had a look of intense terror on her face and jumped backward. At that moment, Dan Beasley tried to make a lunge to get out of the casket, but it turned over and dumped him on the floor. He hit the floor rolling and rolled right against Mrs. Bickley's feet. That time, she jumped both backward, turned around in midair and shot out the door. As she went down Front Street, she was squalling out every breath "like a wild cat whose tail is caught in a barbed wire fence" as Ol' Dad Thomas described it. Mr. Bickley took in right behind her hoping to overtake her. He might have succeeded if she had not glanced around and mistook him for the supposed resurrected corpse. That gave her a new burst of energy.

She ran the full length of Front Street and hit the Tennessee line at full speed. Of course, old Front Street was always full of people, mostly men who frequented the vice dens in that vicinity. Ol' Dad Thomas told me that he was standing in front of Megason's Pool Hall talking to the town sergeant (constable), Mr. John B. Keller. When the screaming woman flew by, she, thinking the ghost was about to overtake her, took time to yell out, "Stop that man!" Mr. Keller, thinking that the Bickleys were having a fight, instantly sprang into action, making a flying tackle and wrapping up Mr. Bickley's ankles, causing him to fall face first on the dirt street. Mr. Bickley's ever-present stovepipe hat sailed from his head and rolled down the street ahead of him. Meanwhile, Mrs. Bickley had reached Major A.D. Reynold's home at 32 Fourth Street. There, she fell onto the front porch, gasping out that a dead man had been chasing her. She did not realize that the "dead man" was her husband, who was then lying in the middle of the street, still held down by John B. Keller, the town sergeant.

But what of Dan Beasley? As soon as he gained his feet over in the funeral parlor, he ran through the railroad yards off toward his home. Once there, he got his wife and, leaving everything behind, raced down to the depot. There, without regard as to what direction the first train was going, he took it. The two were never heard from again.

Yes, friends, if it can happen, it has happened in Bristol.

GHOST IN THE OUTHOUSE

My early welfare work in Bristol often took me to old Poverty Hill. This was a block-long slum on Second High Street located on a low hill in back of and across the tracks from the S.E. Massengill Company, now King Pharmaceuticals. Major A.D. Reynolds had built little "shacks" there as housing for workers in his Fourth Street tobacco processing plant. Within that otherwise solid row of houses, there was a glaring gap. I noticed it immediately on my first visit to the Hill and assumed that one of the shacks had burned down. That was not the case.

By the time I arrived in Bristol (August 1953), the houses on that hill were owned by one or two slum landlords who let them out to various individuals at a modest rate. I soon learned that these humble homes were occupied by poor but very interesting people.

Pictured here is Aunt Betty
Scott, who told of the
ghost in the outhouse and
several other ghost stories.

One of the more interesting residents of Poverty Hill was old Aunt
Betty Scott, who was then (1953) nearing her ninetieth year. Her humble
home was always open to me, and I delighted going there for cheerful
visits. One dark, cold afternoon as I sat by her coal grate fireside, she told
me the story of the mysterious gap that was located directly across the
street from her home.

Way back yander, Tom Collier, who was working in the Reynold's place
[the processing plant], *moved to the little house that stood over there
where the gap is now. His woman* [wife] *was named Birdie. I recollect
her well. They had four or five young-uns and his daddy, who was also
named Tom, Uncle Tom we called him, soon came to live with them.
He was a hateful ol' man, bitter about everything and everybody. They*

said he came home from the Civil War that way and never improved, none. He made life miserable for all of them but they just tolerated him because he had nowhere else to go and young Tom was all he had. Them Collier children were as afraid of him as they would have been a bear cause sometimes, for no reason at all, he would just holler out to Tom or Birdie, "whup them yung-uns good, just beat the devil out of 'em." And then, out in the yard, when Tom or Birdie weren't nearby, he'd just grab hold of one of 'em and make stripes all over, for no cause really. Lot of us here believed he was devil possessed and we believed it more after he died. He got real feeble after he come here but never got passed hobbling out to that little outhouse in the backyard. Ever house up here had one [they still did at that time]. *He'd take his old cob pipe with him and he'd stay out there for hours, no matter how much somebody else needed to go. Sometimes they'd go out there anyway and try to get him out and he'd just holler out and tell them to git outta there, just as harsh and hateful as he could be and if they'd not go right away, he'd push them out talking awful hateful to them.*

It seems that one morning, Old Tom stayed in the outhouse an unusually long time. In fact, he had gone soon after breakfast and had not returned as lunchtime neared. Young Tom was at work, and the children were at school, so Birdie was home alone. She finally ventured out to see about him. As she stepped up to the back door, she was startled to see smoke rolling out between the cracks of the poorly built outhouse. Rushing outside, she threw the door open (he never latched himself in) to find Old Tom engulfed in flames. Apparently he had gone to sleep. His lit pipe had fallen down and set his clothes on fire. Her screams brought out several neighbors, who pulled him into the yard, but it was too late. He was dead, likely because of the smoke he had breathed in. Old Uncle Tom was buried in the Pauper's Section of East Hill Cemetery. Evidently, his spirit did not go with him. Though he was dead and buried, it seems that his ghost came back to further torment his son's family.

"Why that morning after Ol' Uncle Tom's funeral and burial, he was back up here to haint his son and family," Aunt Betty continued on.

Just after daybreak, Birdie made her usual morning trip to the little house in the back. The seat in there showed scorch marks where his clothes had burned and that made her a bit guberish [nervous] *about setting down. But there was no way to put things off so she done it anyhow. But she barely got set down when the smell of pipe smoke filled the place. That alerted her some and in seconds, old icy, bony hands came up from the pit below and pushed up against her bare bottom. And the voice of Old Tom yelled out from that pit, "Git outta here, dad-blast you, git outta here I say!"*

It seems that the ghostly command did not have to be repeated. Aunt Betty shyly described what followed, giggling a bit as she continued her narration. "Why Birdie Collier lept up offa that bench a-hollerin' and a-screachin' real loud and very near knocked the door off the hinges as she lept out into the yard and still doin' what she went in there to do, she frog hopped across the yard right into her kitchen."

Old Birdie must have only remained in that kitchen long enough to adjust her clothes, and then she ran next door, screaming out that a "real haint" was in her outhouse. Now it so happened that the man of the neighboring house was home that morning. Aunt Betty called him "Straight Jim Hamby" and said that he was the "windiest man on the hill, always bragging about his bravery." Doubtless, he was an insecure soul who had to boast of such to prop up a sagging ego (short armchair analysis by this writer).

Aunt Betty continued, "Why Straight Jim always bragged that he wasn't afraid of the devil himself. He avowed that morning that no haint was going to run him out of Collier's outhouse even if there was one in there bigger than Lindamood's bull." Here Aunt Betty explained that a man named Lindamood kept a big old bull in a little pasture, "where that terrible prison was" (she referred to what is now Rotary Field, site of what was a horrible Civil War prison camp; see my book *Between the States* for a description).

Straight Jim, so called because he always stood as straight as a soldier on review, did indeed bravely go to the outhouse. He stepped right in and, as a further display of his professed bravery, dropped the latch in place. Birdie and Straight Jim's wife were cautiously watching from Hamby's back porch, but they had left the kitchen door open for a quick retreat if necessary.

"Well, as I heered it later," Aunt Betty eagerly continued,

that man had barely closed the door when he boldly called out, "Now Old Contrary Tom, do yer damnedest! But yer not going to drive me out of here right quick-like!" Straight Jim held his ground and Birdie was glad for she, like the rest of us, had always heard tell that if one could stand yer ground right before a haint, it would leave and not bother anybody no more. Then, that outhouse began shakin' and bouncin' around like an earthquake had struck it. But Jim stayed on. Still yellin' out, "Go ahead and do it, you ain't a-going to run me outta here." Then things slowed down a bit, and it didn't seem like anything at all was going on in there. It looked like Jim had won.

But if he had won, the victory was temporary. Suddenly, Straight Jim lunged wildly against the outhouse door, knocked it from its hinges, and shot out toward the hill behind the Collier home. He jumped the fence into Lindamood's bull pasture, raced across the field and jumped the back fence, sailing into the brush thicket along what it now Ash Street. As he made his sudden exit, the greatly frightened women had lunged back into the kitchen, slammed and locked the door (as if a locked door could hinder a ghost!) all the while screaming, "It's gonna come out of that pit and likely head straight for here!"

Then Aunt Betty explained what happened by quoting what she had heard Straight Jim tell and explained why he had finally "gave ground," as he expressed it: "I took them bumps and shakes pretty good, but then Ol' Tom just shot up out of that privy hole and started grapping for me with them long bony hands. I didn't have no room to back up, so I just let him have that blamed outhouse!" It seemed that Straight Jim could stand the ghostly sounds but not the ghostly sights.

Then Aunt Betty, leaning back in her ancient rocker and peering into the flickering flames in the coal grate, explained the situation that followed:

Well, sir, them Collier's were in a bad fix. They couldn't get near that old outhouse without that old haint would start a'hollerin' and knockin' and carryin' on something awful. Now it's bad enough having a real haint in the big house, but to have one in your only outhouse is sure troublesome, especially so when the neighbors were backward about having them use theirs for they were afraid that the old haint might follow them Colliers and take up in whatever privy they had to use. They had to start going to the nearby thicket and that was back of Lindamood's bull pasture. Now Birdie was as scared of that big bull as she was the haint and she'd have to go way around the pasture a far piece to the thicket. She'd say to me that she was just about cut off from going with a haint and a bull both in the way.

Now Old Major [Major A.D. Reynolds] said he'd build them another, and he done it but that didn't get rid of the haint. It was right thar in the new one! Guess he should have not built it right on the same pit. Them Colliers left here then, and soon another worker came in and left in a day or two. After that, nobody'd ever live there for to top it all, that bad haint got to poppin' up in the house also. That was right in front of me, here and I got sort of worried about it and scared it might come over here but it didn't. I guess that house stood there vacant for a year or more. Folks claimed they'd see dim lights in there and hear knockin' and so on, but I never did. Then the strangest thing happened. This whole town talked about it for years. One hot afternoon, late, it come up an awful bad cloud in the southwest and there was the awfulest storm that ever was. You know, sir, that storm just swept that house and the outhouse right off the ground and piled them both right over in the fence of Lindamood's pasture right on that bull and killed him dead as a wedge! It looked like the Lord was taking care of both of Birdie's problems even if she had done moved off. What was so strange was that it didn't do a bit of damage to any of the other houses up here. Mighty strange, I always thought. Now, sir, Old Major never did build anything back on that lot and that's why you see that gap over there now.

And so, entertaining as it was, the mystery of the gap was solved. That gap still remained until the entire lot was cleared out several years ago.

THE MAN WHO STOPPED HIS OWN FUNERAL

Far back, a man lived here in Bristol who purely detested funerals. Possibly this was the result of an extreme fear of death. Funerals, of course, were a constant reminder that such does eventually happen to all, and this was a persistent reminder of his own certain demise. Long before his death, he made his family promise not to have a church or home funeral for him. "If anything has to be said, just let it be done up in the cemetery," he would say. "Let it be done real quick-like," he instructed his wife and children.

Finally, the funeral-hating man died. True to his wishes, the family planned a short graveside service for him to be held just before noon. The exact date has been forgotten, but Ol' Dad Thomas remembered that it was in mid-October. He recalled that the day was cloudless, bright and balmy. The deceased only had a few friends and no close relatives, other than his immediate family. So the crowd that gathered for his last rites was very small. In those days, the casket was not suspended over the open grave for the final words, as is done now, but rather it was set on top of the outer case (the box) at the graveside. The preacher secured for this service was very young, barely out of his teens. The family chose him because they thought he wouldn't know much to talk about and would keep the service very short, as requested by the deceased. Indeed, it was a short service. Likely, one of the shortest, if not the shortest, ever held in East Hill.

The family, along with the small crowd, stood on the side of the grave where the casket was located. A few stood on the opposite side. Among the latter was Ol' Dad Thomas, who rarely missed a funeral of local citizens, whether he knew that person or not. Hear what happened as told to this writer more than fifty years ago:

The ghost of a dead man stopped his own funeral near this scene in Bristol's historic East Hill Cemetery.

That strip of a preacher—he were tall and bright red-headed, hadn't said a half a dozen words until one of the dead man's little sons, who wasn't paying much attention to what was being said but were looking around all over the graveyard, screeched out, "Why yander comes Pa." Then one of the older boys called out, "Sure as the devil it is." Well I looked and all of them people looked and sure enough, that dead man were coming right down through the graveyard. Oh, it was a sight. There were black smoke a-puffin' out of his mouth and nose and ears with streaks of fire mixed with it. Folks around here thought he was already burning in torment. Well, sir, that strip of a boy preacher let a yelp and jumped plum across that open grave and took off across the tan-yard holler just a leaping like a chased deer and a-yellin' every breath. Well, them people over there broke and scattered like a bunch of chickens that a big hawk had just been to. Blessed Becky, if they didn't knock that coffin over and the lid flew open and that dead man fell right down in the grave. That coffin fell right on top of him. Yes sir, I seed this happen with my own eyes. By that time, all that bunch was a-tearin' off in every direction, even that dead man's old Aunt Belle. Oh, she was powerful old, but she was outrunnin' that whole bunch. I tore off, too, because I didn't want to be left alone with that smokin' haint after me!

It was clear that Dad Thomas was a bit embarrassed by admitting that he had also fled. But after a brief pause, he finished the story:

Well sir, I reckon that smokin' haint scared the preaching idea plum out of that boy's head. He quit cold that day, never did preach another sermon. Finally, he got to be one of the wildest bucks in town. Wound up down there in Little Hell, a boot-leggin', a-gamblin' and doing all kinds of bad stuff. There was nobody left to do the bare. Late that day, Mayor Terry [Captain John F. Terry] hired a couple rough necks off of Loafer's Glory to go up and finish the job. But he had to liquor them up good before they'd do it for they'd done heard of that smoking ghost up there. Later, one of them got to drinkin' bad and told me private-like that they just throwed the box in on top of the coffin and didn't have much room for dirt. I reckon that's the only man up there who's buried under his coffin instead of in it.

The family of that man soon left Bristol, leaving the grave unmarked. It is now lost. Dad Thomas once showed me the general area but could not locate the exact spot.

THE HOWDY GHOST OF VINEGAR HILL

When I had written about the "bloody foot ghost" previously, I said it was one of the strangest I have heard. This story was telephoned to me from a lady in Marion, Virginia, and her father had directly experienced it.

Vinegar Hill is a section of road a few miles out of Bristol, Tennessee. I often wondered how this strange name had been attached to this particular place. Having heard several accounts as to the naming, I do believe this lady's father was indeed the man responsible.

Far back, folks living out in the Holston Valley would bring produce into town to sell. It is a rather prosperous farming area with good soil, making

The man who first encountered the "Howdy Ghost" is pictured here with his family. The ghost was the cause of the naming of Vinegar Hill in Holston Valley, Sullivan County, Tennessee.

it conducive for the production of many types of crops. Produce of about every kind has been hauled from that valley into Bristol for people to sell to individuals in their homes, along the street or to sometimes barter with local merchants for goods. Sometimes, with professional people, produce was bartered for services rendered.

One old fellow living out that way had made a barrel of vinegar and decided he would haul it to Bristol to sell. He was an early riser and thought he would get a very early start to town, leaving home before daylight. Stars were still twinkling above when he began his journey into the city. As he traveled along, he came upon a long, sloping hill that some folks dreaded when the wagons were full, as it was a bit hard for the animals to pull up the long slope. As he moved slowly up that hill, urging his horses onward, his ear caught a small sound of a voice. The faint voice seemed to be coming from high in the air over his head. It became a bit louder and was calling, "Howdy…howdy…howdy." The horses caught the sound and, frightened, began to run. I have always been told that animals can sense ghosts even before people. Maybe this was the case here. The man tried to stop the horses from running but was unsuccessful. The horses ran on, even though it was a steep incline. He could do nothing with them. The sound was becoming louder and louder, all around him now. Back, front, above, below, the voice was calling out, "Howdy…howdy… howdy." During this event, the large vinegar barrel slid out of the wagon, hit the ground and rolled back down the hill, missing the curve at the bottom of the hill and smashed straight against a tree at the roadside, with the contents completely lost. The man didn't realize that his cargo was lost until he finally got his horses under control a half-mile down the road.

The loss of the vinegar caused by the ghost created an unusual place name in the Holston Valley. We yet call it Vinegar Hill. Well, has this ghost ever been heard from again? Yes, and recently.

Several years ago, a man walking along that very stretch of the road in broad daylight began to hear a voice over him calling out, "Howdy… howdy…howdy," becoming louder and louder as he walked along. You may be sure that the walk turned into a run! He was asked how far the ghost followed him. He didn't really know because, as he said, he was running so fast that he was concentrating on getting away instead of listening for the voice. He later admitted that his hands were over his ears to drown out the eeriness.

Another fellow had a similar experience walking home along the road in the night after "courting" in the valley. In the darkness of the night, a voice, faintly at first but growing louder out of the heavens, began to call, "Howdy…howdy…howdy." Now this man didn't hesitate but rather ran at the first sound, heading very quickly down the road. Alas, he missed a turn in that road and dead-centered a large tree (maybe the same tree against which the vinegar barrel burst). This knocked him completely out. When he came to, it was daylight and the sound had ceased.

Another man, driving along the road in an automobile, suddenly had his car stop on that hill with no explanation. The voice began to come from above: "Howdy…howdy…howdy." This man abandoned his car and ran. He would not go back to see about it until daylight.

Who knows? If you go by that spot at night or even in daylight, you may be greeted by what I call the "Howdy ghost."

THE METHODIST MISSION GHOST

Ghosts have been known to do many things, but seldom do we hear of one that stops a promising mission effort. That once happened in Bristol. I have long contended that if anything could happen it has happened in Bristol, and here is more proof of that.

In 1882, the Main Street Methodist Church of Bristol, Virginia (now known as State Street Methodist), decided to start mission work in west Bristol. The effort soon met with a measure of success that was far beyond the most optimistic expectations. From a humble beginning in a former residential dwelling, the group soon erected a one-room building with plans for additions to be made in the near future. A semiretired Methodist minister was engaged to be the temporary pastor. Every passing Sunday saw an increase in attendance. Old Main Street Church was well pleased with the progress, having plans for greater financial aid in the year 1883.

Soon after the mission was set up, an old lady whom everyone called "Aunt Meldie" began attending every service offered by this new work. She was a widow with no family and practiced a rather lively form of worship. Some of the Methodists were rather lively in those days. Living just across the street, she could easily hear the spirited singing of the group, and this is what drew her in. She soon noticed that one thing was

Old State Street Church, located in downtown Bristol, Virginia, started a mission church that was stopped by a ghost.

missing—no instrument was present. Now, Aunt Meldie loved music and had in her home a rather new pump organ that she had learned to play well. She had the organ moved over to the mission, with the stipulation that she could play it anytime she wished between services. It was soon learned that she was the only one in the congregation who could play, so she was made church organist.

Those folks attending that mission dearly loved the music that the old lady was able to pump out of that fine organ—so much so that they soon had her playing a medley of old songs for perhaps fifteen minutes before the actual service began. It was felt that this created a spiritual mood conducive to a better service to follow. Aunt Meldie delighted to do it.

About three months after the organ was moved to the church, there was an especially lively morning service. Aunt Meldie pumped much longer and harder than usual and in a very vigorous manner. Then, after a long and highly emotional service by the pastor, Aunt Meldie took the stool to play a closing hymn. During that hymn, the music just suddenly stopped, for Aunt Meldie had fallen to the floor, mortally stricken with either a stroke or a heart attack. Within seconds, she was gone.

It was a very sad group that came together on the following Sunday. Folks talked in low tones, and grief hung over that place like a pall. About fifteen minutes before the service was to start, those sitting on the front pews were startled when the organ lid slid upward and backward with not a soul near it. The pedals then began to make their rhythmic up and down motions with no earthly feet on them. A sad funeral hymn peeled forth from that organ, and the style was unmistakably that of the recently deceased Aunt Meldie. One fearful and ultrasuperstitious old sister sitting near the front set off the panicky stampede by yelling out, "Lord have mercy, thar's a haint playin' that organ!" No one knows how long the organ played because in minutes there was no one left to hear it. The building and the grounds were cleared out in record time.

Next Sunday, the crowd was very small. Only a few brave souls who were determined to continue on ventured into the mission building. It was noticed that even they sat far away from the organ. They soon were much farther away when that organ began playing right on schedule and without the benefit of Aunt Meldie.

On the following Sunday, no one showed up for the service. It was apparent that if the mission was to continue, the greatly feared organ would have to go. After the mission leaders and the official board of the Main Street Methodist Church agreed to do this, another problem developed. Aunt Meldie had no heirs to whom the organ could be given (that is, if anyone would have taken a haunted organ). Finally, it was given to a family not connected to the mission who knew nothing of the story. That family ended up dragging the instrument to the back of a cow pasture near their home and dumping it in a ditch the very next day. It had spent only one night in the home. That was long enough, for about midnight it had peeled forth with sad funeral music. The family had no member present who could even play the instrument and quickly fled.

Meanwhile, leaders of the mission made sure that word passed around that the haunted organ had been removed from the building and that all was well. The message was well received and apparently served its purpose. The following Sunday saw the little building filled to capacity with a congregation that was eager to continue what had become a flourishing mission work. But alas, about fifteen minutes before the service was to begin, there came from the corner, where Aunt Meldie and the organ had sat, the sad funeral music from an organ that wasn't even there. Apparently, ghosts do not need an earthly instrument to make unearthly sounds! The little building was vacated faster than before. In fact, many in the panicky crowd did not wait for the one door to be cleared but rather jumped from the windows and made a hasty retreat. That crowd never assembled again. The consensus of opinion was that one could move a haunted organ but could not move a stubborn ghost.

The mission effort ceased. In all my collection of strange stories I have been told, this is the only instance of a church being disbanded because of a ghost.

ABOUT THE AUTHOR

B ud Phillips has been a resident of Bristol, Virginia, since 1953. He first began to hear strange and unique stories about the past from his older clients when he served as a social worker. In March 2006, he began writing a detailed history column for the sesquicentennial celebrations of Bristol, and due to popular demand he continues to write for the *Bristol Herald Courier* to this day. Now, yielding to request and pressure, he has decided to fill the need for a collection of ghost tales.

Included in this work is an extensive sampling of the many and varied ghost tales that have been shared with Bud Phillips over the past fifty-seven years. In this presentation are tales stretching from the remote past to the present time. They have come from a wide cross section of Bristolians—from the obscure to professionals and leading business people. The stories vary from the deadly serious to the light and humorous. Phillips presents them solely because of public demand.

Visit us at
www.historypress.net